FINGER LAKES
ALMANAC

A Guide to the Natural Year

FINGER LAKES ALMANAC

A Guide to the Natural Year

Margaret Miller

Illustrated by Sheri Amsel

FINGER LAKES ALMANAC
A Guide to the Natural Year

Text Copyright 2005
by
Margaret Miller

Illustrations Copyright 2005
by
Sheri Amsel

ISBN 0-925168-96-3

Library of Congress Cataloging-in-Publication Data

Miller, Margaret.
Finger Lakes almanac : a guide to the natural year / by Margaret Miller ; illustrations by Sheri
Amsel.
p. cm.
ISBN 0-925168-96-3 (alk. paper)
1. Natural history—New York (State)—Finger Lakes. 2. Finger Lakes (N.Y.) I. Amsel, Sheri.
II. Title.
QH105.N4M46 2004
508.747'8—dc22
2004021477

NORTH COUNTRY BOOKS, INC.
311 Turner Street
Utica, New York 13501

Table of Contents

Introduction

Surrounded by a rich diversity of flora, fauna, and landscapes, the nine thousand some acres of the Finger Lakes Region of Central New York State are a real treasure. The topography, carved out by glaciers during the Ice Age, varies widely, from gently rolling hills and lush forests, to ravines, gorges, and waterfalls. The area is a haven for nature lovers and outdoor enthusiasts during any season.

There are many new and exciting changes in the natural world of the Finger Lakes throughout the year. Whether your interest is birds, rainbows, or the weather, you'll find a wide assortment of interesting examples here.

Because of the effect this unique collection of lakes has upon the weather, the Finger Lake region is well suited for the cultivation of grapes. Vineyards cover the slopes which are home to a number of wineries.

In *Finger Lakes Almanac*, I have focused on what I feel to be some of the more interesting tidbits of information regarding the amazing natural world of the Finger Lake region throughout the calendar year.

JANUARY

January is usually a cold, snowy month in the Finger Lakes Region. Unless you are a skier, a snowmobiler or an ice fisherman, you may want to just curl up with a good book before the fire and try to escape "cabin fever," yet a moonlit January night may give the "luster of mid-day" and entice you to break out the down parka and fur-lined mittens, pull on the insulated boots and go out for a walk.

Most years, but not all, there is a warm spell, the "January thaw," which melts some snow and ice, and sets the little creeks gurgling in glee.

Birds

January is a harsh month for the birds that spend their winters around the Finger Lakes, especially for the smaller species, such as chickadees, finches, and nuthatches. The days are short, so they don't have very much time to search for food when they need it most. At the same time, the nights are long so they are forced to go without nourishment for longer periods.

Birds have a high metabolism and need to consume an amount of food equal to their body weight each day. If there is a sudden, substantial reduction in the amount of food available, their body temperatures will drop, which is potentially fatal. To compensate, they reduce their activity. Once they find a food source, they seldom travel very far from it.

Birds often visit backyard feeders. If you start feeding these avian visitors,

1

it is important to have food in the feeder at all times. If birds unexpectedly find their food supply gone, they may perish before they can locate another.

Birdwatchers get a lot of enjoyment watching birds at their feeders. It's a special thrill when an unexpected species shows up. Around the Finger Lake region, most of the birds you see are seed-eaters: black-capped chickadees, cardinals, white-breasted nuthatches, tufted titmice, blue jays, evening grosbeaks, cedar waxwings, to name a few. Sometimes there are winter visitors from the north: redpolls, crossbills, white-crowned and white-throated sparrows, among others. Then there are the suet-eaters; the woodpeckers: downy, hairy, and less often, the red-bellied. You may also see hawks, most likely red-tailed, red-shouldered, or a coopers, swoop down and snatch one of the small birds.

To survive frigid winter nights, birds fluff their feathers and huddle together on their perches. Sometimes it is on a branch near the trunk of a dense evergreen, sometimes in a sheltered former nesting box. Birds turn their heads and tuck their bills under their feathers and sleep on their roosts.

It is extremely rare for any of the larger and deeper Finger Lakes to freeze over during the winter. Therefore, many species, of ducks congregate in "rafts," groups of several dozen or more, and float on the water quite near the shore. One of the best places to see a great variety of them is on Cayuga Lake in the Sheldrake area where mallards, black ducks, scaup, buffelheads, American golden-eyes, canvasbacks, redheads, mergansers, and other species spend their days waiting for the arrival of spring.

A World Covered in Snow —the Crows

There are a lot of crows around the Finger Lakes. In January, these large jet-black birds really stand out in a world covered with snow. About nineteen inches in length, with a wingspan of thirty-six inches and loud raucous calls, they are not low profile.

The common short-billed crow is native to the temperate region of north Florida to the arctic coast, and west to the plains. Related to the raven, the blue jay, the rook, and the jackdaw, of the Corvidae family, crows mate in early spring. They build large stick nests in tall trees. The female sits on the green-spotted eggs; the male provides food.

Crows form tight family bonds and spend months, sometimes years with their parents. In the wild, crows are both scavengers and predators. They feed on carrion, frogs, toads, salamanders, small snakes, mice, beetles, June bugs, caterpillars, cutworms, fruits, and seeds. They also steal other birds' nests.

Because they pull up and eat sprouting corn, crows don't win any popularity contests among farmers. At one time farmers planted tarred corn seed to deter them. They also shot them. However, many farmers will tell you that a crow's judgment of the range of a particular gun is right on target.

Normally a crow flies at the rate of twentyfive to thirty miles per hour. Its maximum speed is sixty miles per hour.

Crows do not migrate. Throughout the winter you often see them perched on bare tree branches.

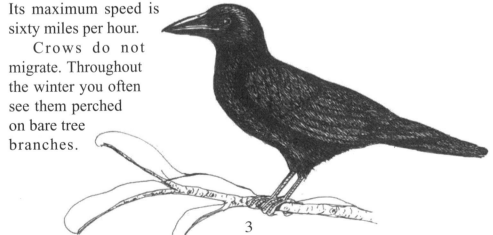

3

You can hear them, too. Their short, repeated caws are their standard territorial language. If a predator—a hawk or an owl—appears, a crow's call is a more drawn out "aurgh" that brings out other crows in defense. Under their attack, the would-be predator retreats.

Around the Finger Lakes, we have a slightly smaller crow than the common crow: the fish crow or bonebreaker. It eats mostly fish that have died and washed ashore. It also raids the nests of shore birds.

Ornithologists believe the crow is more intelligent, more clever and more sociable that any other member of the bird family.

A Beaver's Life

By January the ponds and swamps of the Finger Lakes are usually frozen over, their surfaces covered with a carpet of snow. On some of them you may see large, domed structures made of sticks and mud: beaver lodges. The landscape appears to be devoid of life. However, there is a lot of activity that doesn't meet the eye. While many insects and amphibians are sleeping the winter away burrowed into the mud bottoms of the ice-covered ponds, beavers do not hibernate. In mid to late January, beavers are beginning their breeding season. It will be in full swing early to mid February. After the mating season ends, beavers resume their usual routine of eating, resting, and sleeping.

The state mammal of New York, the beaver is the largest rodent in North America, reaching up to forty-five inches in length, including its tail, and weighing as much as fifty pounds. Its hind feet are large and webbed for swimming. The front feet are small and hand-like, and are used for carrying things. The second toe on each hind foot has a double claw that the animal uses to comb its fur. Like other rodents, its brain is small for its size and lacks the abundant convolution of human brains that are believed to be an indication of intelligence. The Indians, however, credited beavers with great intelligence.

Smart or not, beavers know the advantages of living and working together. And their engineering skill is legendary. Choosing a site in a slow-moving forest stream, they construct dams of sticks and mud. They gnaw down aspen, birch, poplar, and willow trees, drag and float them to a selected spot, where they bury the tips of the branches in mud with the ends pointing upstream. They continue to fit more saplings together, adding more mud until a strong barrier is completed. Their dams are purposely not watertight; there must be enough water flowing through to keep it from becoming stagnant, while at the same time creating a pond in which the water level will remain pretty much constant so the beaver house, or lodge, can be fitted to it.

The domed-shaped lodge is built of sticks, brush, and mud, and constructed much like the dam. Inside, it may by three feet high and ten feet in diameter. Before winter, the beavers plaster the outside with a thick coat of mud. There are two levels in the structure so the animals will be protected in case the water level rises. The entrance hole is below the thickest ice that may cover the pond in winter.

It seldom gets below freezing in a beaver's lodge; the thick walls keep out the bitter cold. Little outside air seeps in, reducing the beaver's supply of oxygen. Therefore, their activities are slowed.

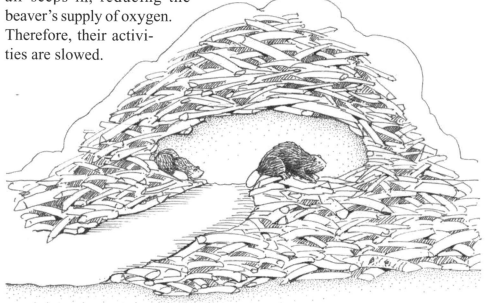

5

Where food is plentiful, large colonies of beaver often live together in a sort of beaver village. It is believed they mate for life. Each family has its own house, but they all join forces to defend the colony if necessary. If the dam needs repair, they all share the work. Members of the colony also take care of babies that become orphaned.

Beavers are peaceful animals, affectionate among themselves. The kittens, or cubs, are born in April. Usually four or five in number, there is but one litter a year. The newborns' eyes are open at birth. Within two weeks they are able to swim about with their mother. They remain in the family home, along with their parents and yearling kits, until they are two and one-half years old.

Toward fall of the second year, the young male beaver starts out to establish a new home or a colony if the one into which he was born has become too crowded. Usually it will be within about six miles of his parents. Upon finding a suitable location, he digs a burrow into a bank, starting below the surface of the water, and slants it up to a small two-level room above the high water level. The beavers' first litter will be born in this starter home. The following autumn, the parents will build their large, permanent lodge.

In the fall, after the beavers have finished their homes, they harvest and store their winter food supply. They feed mostly on the bark, twigs, and leaves of the same aspen, birch, and willows they use to build their homes. They often gnaw down whole stands of them, cut the trees into shorter lengths, bring them to the pond, often through canals they have dug previously, and sink them near their lodges.

Beavers are exceedingly hard workers, but after a fall of unceasing labor, they are content to spend a quiet winter in their warm, dry lodges, swimming out only to get a branch from their cache which they bring home to munch on inside.

A beaver has the special physical equipment to implement his engineering skills: strong jaws with well-developed front teeth that have thin, chiseled edges. Orange in color, the teeth grow continually to compensate for constant wear. The beavers are excellent swimmers and divers, and can remain under water for up to eleven minutes. Their ten-to-eighteen-inch long, broad, flat tails act as rudders and serve as props when they sit upright. When danger threatens, the beaver will slap its tail loudly on the water as a signal to other members of the colony to scuttle to the safety of their dens.

The beaver's rich brown fur is beautiful. With long outer hairs and thick, soft underfur, it is also exceptionally warm. In the seventeenth, eighteenth, and early nineteenth centuries, there was an insatiable market for the pelts in Europe.

From the mid-1600s until as late as 1820, a beaver hide was a "coin of the realm." For one pelt, a trapper could get a half pound of wampum, a pound of shot, five pounds of sugar, a pound of tobacco, 25 fishhooks, or twelve buttons. Six hides bought a blanket and twenty bought a gun.

With a beaver trapper's average daily income about 32 times that of a farm laborer, it's not surprising the animals faced extinction. Even after the price of a beaver hide fell by about five hundred percent in the 1840s, roughly 500,000 of the animals were being taken each year, mostly for their fur. However, some were killed to get castoram, the most widely used animal product in perfume, which came from their glands.

By the late nineteenth century, many Americans began to worry that beavers would be totally wiped out, so they enacted laws to protect them; slowly their numbers increased.

It has been estimated that beavers have been around for 35 million years. You can find them now in many of the wildlife areas around the Finger Lakes, including the Finger Lakes National Forest near Hector, The Connecticut Hill Wildlife Management Area in Schuyler County, the Cummins Nature Center near Naples, and in the Montezuma National Wildlife Refuge at the north end of Cayuga Lake. They have also taken up residence on private property throughout the area.

The best time to observe beavers is at dusk. They are most active from sundown to sunup.

The January Night Sky

Many people in the Finger Lakes region don't look forward to the long, cold, dark January evenings. The north wind howls, and the roads are often slippery, making travel hazardous. Many of the wild creatures are inactive; there doesn't seem to be much that's appealing in the outside world in January. It's tempting to curl up before the fire with a good book.

However, there are also moonlit evenings when the beauty of the moon shining on a snow-blanketed landscape is breathtaking. The Iroquois Indians who inhabited the Finger Lakes Region gave each full moon a name. January was known as the Wolf Moon; February, the Snow Moon; March, the Sap or Worm Moon; April, the Pink Moon; May, the Flower Moon. They called June, the Hot or Strawberry Moon; July, the Buck Moon; August, the Sturgeon Moon. September was the Harvest or Corn Moon; October, the Hunter's Moon; November, the Beaver Moon; and December, the Cold Moon.

A full moon occurs about every twenty-seven and one-third days. Therefore, some years we have thirteen. Perhaps that is why the Iroquois had more than one name for some of them. The second full moon in a month is called a Blue Moon.

But it is when the night is dark and the atmosphere clear that the January night sky is most interesting. To go out and look up at the infinite vault of heaven glittering over your head is like entering a fairyland. During January, there are more brilliant stars in view than at any other time of the year. Of the earth's twenty brightest stars, fifteen are visible in the skies over the Finger Lakes and ten spangle the firmament during the coldest months. Each fiery point seems to sparkle, or twinkle, in the density of frosty air, but actually stars do not twinkle at all, the effect of the earth's atmosphere gives that appearance. If you were in a spaceship outside the atmosphere, you would see them shine with a clear, steady light.

Sirius is the brightest and most beautiful star in the winter night sky. On nights of unsteady atmosphere, it shoots rays of ruby, sapphire, white, and emerald like a miniature Fourth of July skyrocket. This is most spectacular when viewed through binoculars or a telescope. Sirius is so bright partly because it is quite near the earth, astronomically speaking—eight and one-half light years—and because it is orbited by a smaller white star.

Stars are classified by magnitude according to their brightness: the brighter the star, the lower the magnitude. With the naked eye you can see roughly two to three thousand individual stars. Those below fifth magnitude are not visible without optical aids. Billions of stars compose the Milky Way — Jacob's Ladder, Galaxy, and Pathway of Souls among them — the hazy band that stretches overhead from horizon to horizon.

Constellations are groups of stars which always present the same appearance when viewed from earth. Named by the ancients after shapes they fancied they saw in the heavens, the choice of names suggests the practice began in Mesopotamia. The animals for which some of the constellations are named were native to that area. Later, the Greeks added names of their heroes and demigods. The Romans took the Greek list and translated the names to Latin, the "official" names we use today.

Most of the major constellations have one or more stars of first magnitude or second. An exception is the unmistakable Pleiades, or Seven Sisters, a group of closely clustered stars in Taurus in the hump of the "bull's" shoulder. With the naked eye you can see six or seven stars; with binoculars, twenty; with a telescope, two hundred. The poet Tennyson described the Pleiades as "glittering, like a swarm of fireflies."

Dominating the January night sky is Orion, the largest, most brilliant and most beautiful constellation in the heavens. If you draw an imaginary line around him, you will see eight of the most brilliant stars in the sky.

We can all identify the Big Dipper (part of Ursa Major) and the two pointers on the outside edge of the Dipper in a direct line with the North Star (Pole star, Polaris), the guiding light of ancient travelers, and which is almost exactly above the earth's North Pole. Polaris and the two pointers are second magnitude stars. Ursa Major, Ursa Minor, Cassiopeia, Perseus, and Draco are grouped around Polaris. Circumpolar, they never rise or set, and are visible throughout the year. All other major constellations appear to rise and set like the moon.

In January, Orion rises in the early evening, and is overhead at midnight. It will slip to the west as the season progresses. This mighty hunter of Greek legend has a dog following at his heels; Sirius is the star in the dog's collar. Ranged across Orion in a diagonal are three stars, which form Orion's belt. Hanging from his belt is his sword — a line of fainter stars.

To locate the constellations, you will probably need a sky map. They are available at planetariums, the astronomy departments of universities, and at many bookstores. If you have ocular aids, look for the famous Orion Nebula, a cloud of glowing gases where stars are "born." You've probably seen photos of the Nebula, taken through telescopes, on posters or other places where there are astronomical scenes.

Stars, which we see as tiny dots in the heavens, are actually monstrous globs of extremely hot glowing gas; in other words, suns. They look so small only because they are so far away. Our sun has a diameter of 864,000 miles, and is 92.9 million miles away. Sirius is three times as large but is 51 trillion miles distant.

Stars differ in color. Using instruments known as spectroscopes, scientists can tell from its color what elements are in a star. Bluish-white helium stars are the youngest and the hottest; red the coolest and oldest.

When stargazing, you may see a meteor flash across the sky. In the Finger Lakes region in early January, you may see an increased number of them on the night of the Quandrantid meteor shower.

Any night you might also see a meteor or meteorite. Meteorites make contact with the earth's surface, whereas meteors burn up in the atmosphere, their brilliant tails seen across the night sky. Both are particles of cosmic dust heated to incandescence by their swift descent through the earth's atmosphere.

If you study the relatively dim star Algol in the constellation Perseus through binoculars, you will see that its light intensity varies every three days. Algol is one of the more dramatic of the many stars with eclipsing binaries, "companion" stars which circle about them and get between them and the earth, causing a partial eclipse. The ancients feared looking at Algol, believing it to be an evil star because it winked at them.

Resembling stars are the eight planets which traverse the skies over the Finger Lakes. However, whereas stars are burning balls of gases, planets are solid, and the light they give off is not their own, but reflected from the sun. The planets are much closer to us than the stars, and the beams of light they send us are so broad that atmospheric effect is not noticeable.

Unlike the stars which appear to be "fixed" in the heavens, the planets are vagabonds. They are not always in the same position in the night sky. One may appear in the east as a brilliant morning "star;" and sometimes in the west as the evening "star." Venus, Mars, Jupiter, Saturn, and Mercury are visible to the naked eye at various times of the year but you'll need a telescope to see Uranus, Neptune, and Pluto. Use an up-to-date almanac to give you the planets' locations.

January nights may be long, dark, and cold here in the Finger Lakes, but there are still things to light up your life.

An Abundance of Snow

In January, snow is a given around the Finger Lakes. How much, how early, or how late depends on the season and where you are. According to the National Weather Service, the average yearly snowfall in both Auburn and Skaneateles is about 92"; in Bath, 46". Elmira gets 43"; Geneva 61", and Ithaca about 70".

We've all been told that no two snowflakes are alike, but when you consider the number of snowflakes that fall to make up the aforementioned totals, it's mind-boggling. Without question, the variety of the beautiful forms

11

of snowflakes is infinite. W.A. Bently, a meteorologist born in Vermont, was the first person to photograph these ice crystals, and took pictures of more than 1,000 of them.

A snowflake is simply a minute ice-shaped crystal. Some are flat, others tubular, columnar needles. One thing all of them have in common is that they all have six sides or angles. Those formed in low clouds are usually large and branching; those in high clouds are smaller and compact.

Contrary to the scenes on Christmas cards that invariably show snowflakes gently falling, that's not how it always is. There are snow squalls, brief but intense snowstorms with gusty winds that can wipe out your visibility in an instant. Then there are blizzards which are intense and dangerous storms. To be designated as a blizzard, a snowfall has to be heavy and accompanied by howling winds of at least 35 mph, with temperatures of twenty degrees or less for an extended period of time, and with visibility of less than one-quarter of a mile. Most years only a very few blizzards blast through the Finger Lakes; some years, none at all.

When weather forecasters predict "heavy snow," it means they expect four to eight inches of snow will fall in the next twelve hours, and as much as six inches or more in the next 24 hours. Often there is, of course, some margin of error in these forecasts.

It takes about ten inches of snow to equal one inch of water. Walking through only six inches of snow takes as much effort as walking two miles on bare ground. Packed snow begins to squeak underfoot when the thermometer registers about five degrees Fahrenheit.

During clear weather when the ground is covered with snow, the temperature on the ground in evergreen-wooded areas is typically five degrees warmer than where there is bare snowy ground. That is because the dark-colored evergreens absorb sunlight and radiate it as heat whereas bare snowy ground reflects most of the sunlight.

Snow on the hills of the Finger Lakes in late winter will remain on the ground for another ten days, for each 300 feet in elevation.

Because it contains a great amount of air, snow is an exceedingly poor conductor of heat, therefore, it is a good insulator. A blanket of snow is essential to protect the dormant vegetation in the Finger Lakes region.

FEBRUARY

Traditionally February is the coldest month of the year around the Finger Lakes. Snow and ice cover the land. However, daylight lingers a bit longer than it did a month or so ago. A great variety of birds appear at backyard feeders and, speaking of birds, great-horned owls are beginning to nest and vocalize. Their rather spooky, "Whoo-whoo-whoo" can be heard for up to a mile through the quiet, cold air.

Whistle-Pigs and Phil

February weather is harsh around the Finger Lakes. However, there is an occasional spring-like day, and daylight lingers a bit longer now. One resident of the area, the woodchuck, sometimes called groundhog, is still sound asleep deep in his underground burrow. A true hibernator, he will not emerge until early April, Punxsutawney Phil notwithstanding.

Light to medium brown and about the size of a house cat but more thick-bodied, the woodchuck has legs so short its belly sometimes drags on the ground. It is the third largest rodent, after the beaver and porcupine, in North America. Its eyes, nose, and ears are close to the top of its head so it can see, smell, and hear with only its crown sticking out of its burrow, though you often see one standing up, looking around and sniffing the air. The distinctive whistle sound it makes accounts for why it is also commonly called a "whistle-pig."

Woodchucks dig their own burrows or enlarge one that has been used by foxes. The average length is about fourteen feet. Burrows are often located on open, rolling hillsides or along a hedgerow or the edge of a woods; always where there is an adjoining open field to provide both food and security. The entrance hole is large so the animal can run in and turn around. There is also a smaller "spy" hole, dug from the inside so there is no visible loose dirt around it. There is always a separate chamber for excrement.

A woodchuck's front teeth are broad and chisel-shaped for gnawing, rather than sharp and pointed for tearing flesh like those of the carnivores. The woodchuck sits up on its haunches to clutch a stem of clover in its front paws while feeding. In late summer the woodchuck eats almost constantly, putting on the layer of fat that will keep it alive during the winter.

By the time frost has killed its food supply—late September or early October—it is asleep in its burrow. Usually, it will not use its summer burrow but a different one on the edge of a woodlot, in a clump of briers, a hedgerow, or a patch of sumac. It curls up, tucks its nose between its hind legs and feet, and gradually goes to sleep. Little by little its heartbeat drops about ninety-five percent, from eighty beats per minute down to four or five. The animal's oxygen consumption falls also. Its summer respiration rate of thirty to forty breaths per minute drops to only one breath every six minutes. Its temperature falls from about 96.8° to about 38°.

The chucks awake in early March, occasionally in late February if the weather has been unseasonably warm. A male wastes no time in searching for a mate. He wanders about systematically checking other burrows for a receptive female.

15

Sometimes he is chased away by the female or by another male that got there first.

Copulation takes place in the burrow; the mated pair usually lives together until just before the young are born. An old male may go to the female's burrow, remain a short time, and then return to his own burrow. He visits her several times a day. Usually a woodchuck has but one mate a year.

The mating burrow is where the young are born after an approximately twenty-eight to thirty-three day gestation period. The brood chamber is about fourteen inches high, sixteen inches wide and is lined with fine dried grass.

At birth the four to five chucklings are approximately four inches long and weigh about an ounce. At twenty-eight days their eyes open; and at six weeks they venture out into the sunlight. They are about ten inches long and weigh about half a pound. The male has no part in raising them.

Once out of the den, the chucklings are forced by their mother to eat green plants, and soon they are nibbling clover and alfalfa — loved above all else by woodchucks.

Many young woodchucks fall victim to hawks and red foxes. In mid-July, the survivors leave the family for a territory of their own.

Night Dwellers — the Owls

February is a good month to keep your eyes and ears open for owls. As they are nocturnal, owls are probably the least often seen bird in the Finger Lakes region, though eight different kinds live in or visit the area in the course of a year.

Owls have been used as a symbol of evil or death to anyone who so much as heard their call. The owl was also the symbol of the Greek goddess of wisdom, Athena.

Birds of prey, all owls have some common characteristics. The females are larger than the males. Like humans, they have binocular vision but they cannot move their eyes from side to side. They can, however, rotate their heads three-quarters of the way around. They do this with lightning-quick speed, making it seem as if their heads are completely rotating. They can see in daylight, but at night their pupils dilate almost to the edge of their eyes and they are still able to see with a hundred times less light than humans.

Owls possess the greatest auditory powers of all birds. Their ears are huge, hidden behind feathers on the sides of their heads. On some species the so-called "ears" are tufts of feathers used as an aid in camouflage and for recognition between individuals.

All owls have large feet equipped with consummate weapons: four powerful needle-sharp talons, two at the front, two at the back. They have equally powerful hooked beaks. When they attack, their talons are lowered, much like the landing gear on an airplane. The down-like edges of the wings dampen the sound of a flying owl. The prey never hears the silent hunter.

Usually the prey is killed instantly by the piercing, slashing talons; occasionally the beak delivers the final coup. The prey is then torn into manageable pieces for the bird to eat efficiently

Depending upon their size, owls nest in abandoned crow, hawk, flicker, pileated woodpecker, hawk, or heron nests. Sometimes they use natural cavities in trees. The great-horned owl occasionally evicts the residents of a nest it fancies. Nesting owls are fierce defenders of their domain. It is wise to give them a wide berth.

An owl's digestive system assimilates the nutritious portions of its prey. The rest (hair, bones, claws, teeth, etc.) is regurgitated in the form of pellets. The presence of these pellets under a tree is an indication either of an owl's nest or its favorite perch.

Great Horned Owl

If you are outside in the Finger Lakes region some late February night and hear a deep-pitched, mournful hoot that is repeated three to eight times and is so downright spooky it sends shivers down your spine, there is a great horned owl around. Its call can be heard for over a mile on a still night.

Standing eighteen to twenty-five inches tall, with a wingspan of forty-eight to sixty inches, the great horned owl is our largest, most powerful and most rapacious owl. The female weighs about four pounds and the male about three. He is a few inches shorter as well. Fluffed with feathers, both appear much larger than they really are. One of the largest birds of prey in the world, an adult great horned owl is the ultimate in strength and aggressiveness.

Its name is misleading. What appear as two "horns" on the top of its head are actually long tufts of feathers. However, along with its huge yellow eyes—the largest of any bird—and its stout curved beak, they serve to accentuate the owl's fearsome countenance.

The bird shuns civilization for secluded, dense patches of woodland where its somber plumage blends with its surroundings, especially tree bark. Its most distinguishing mark is a white "collar" around its throat. During the day it dozes motionless on an upper branch of a tree close to the trunk. Telltale pellets alert one to a great horned owl's presence.

The diet of a great horned is eclectic. It prefers rodents and small mammals. Skunk is one of its favorite meals. It will also eat songbirds, game birds, poultry, snakes, and even a cat that strays into its territory.

The ultimate palate pleaser is the brain of a small mammal. Most of the prey taken back to the larder tree is headless.

The great horned's hoot is its territory call. Used to communicate with its mate while hunting, and upon returning from its nightly hunt, the call is often heard just before dawn.

Great horned owls mate for life. During courtship the male tries to impress the female with feather fluffing, head bowing, and a shuffling dance. Then he puts on a show of aerial acrobatics. After much head rubbing, beak snapping, and hooting, they mate. This occurs in late February to March.

The female lays two to three white eggs and begins incubating them as soon as the first two are laid. During incubation, the male is the provider. The owlets hatch a week or more apart. At birth, they are pink and featherless but soon grow coats of white down. They reach full size in ten weeks. By the time they leave the nest in early June, their color is generally a dark brown with black flecks.

The babies have voracious appetites and shriek to express their hunger. Even after they leave the nest but are not yet skilled enough in hunting to feed themselves, they follow their parents around shrieking for food.

Great horned owls do not migrate.

Short-eared Owl

February is a good month to see migratory owls. Raised in the land of the midnight sun, these owls seem to have a hard time telling day from night. Therefore, you may see them in the daytime flying over open fields hunting for rodents, especially field mice.

Short-eared owls are the only diurnal (active during daylight) owls commonly found south of the Arctic. With rounded heads—their feather tufts are small—and bright yellow eyes, they are thirteen to seventeen inches tall and have a wingspan of thirty-nine to forty-four inches. They are hawk-like in appearance and behavior.

While most owls are solitary birds; the short-eared are gregarious. You may come upon a group of them perched together in an evergreen tree. And while most owls are vocal as well, the short-eared are quiet except during breeding season. Because they migrate, we in the Finger Lakes are not privileged to hear their courtship calls.

Snowy Owl

A snowy owl appears only sporadically every few winters around the Finger Lakes. It is a large bird, twenty-one to twenty-five inches long with a wingspan of fifty to sixty inches. You may see a snowy on a fence post, a light pole, or even a highway sign. A few years ago one stayed around the tower at Cornell University for several weeks. Mostly, snowy owls prefer open country. On the wing, they are so fast they can overtake a grouse in flight.

The adult male is almost pure white while the female is heavily flecked with dusky brown.

I haven't found anyone who has ever heard one of these visitors from the north. A turn of the century guide describes its call as "hideous cries, which resemble those of a man in deep distress."

The snowy owl has the distinction of being the earliest known representation of a bird identifiable by species. Its likeness was painted on the ice-age walls of the cave of Les Trois Freres in France.

20

Long-eared Owl

Essentially, long-eared owls, like the short-eared, are winter migrants to the Finger Lakes. Also like the short-eared, you may see several roosting together in an evergreen tree. They prefer dense stands of conifers but are found also in deciduous stands. They are moderate-sized birds approximately fifteen inches tall, and have a wingspan of thirty-six to forty-two inches.

These owls are named for their ear tufts, which are longer than those on other owls of comparable size. Their soft, deep "Hoo-ooo" is not as hair-raising as the calls of most other owls. Though it is rare, a few long-eared nest in higher elevations around the Finger Lakes.

Saw-whet Owl

If you run across one of these captivating little creatures consider yourself extremely fortunate. They are winter visitors to the Finger Lakes where they frequent moist or swampy woodlands or areas close to water.

A few years ago a friend of mine discovered one in a Christmas tree he was cutting near Cayuga Lake. The little fellow was amazingly tame and seemed in no hurry to fly off. Being nocturnal, maybe it just wasn't awake yet.

As owls go, a saw-whet is tiny, weighing a mere four ounces. It is seven-to-eight-inches tall and has a wingspan of about eighteen inches, a wide rounded head and bright yellow eyes. The adult has a brown back with white mottling. The underparts are white with vertical brown stripes. Its call sounds like the rasping of a file sharpening a saw, hence its name.

Saw-whets patrol low over fields and meadows where they can pick up the rustle, squeak, or even the footfall of a mouse or rat, their chief prey.

Barred Owl

With handsomely striped and barred plumage, the barred owl is one of our largest, sixteen to twenty-three inches tall with wings that stretch thirty-eight to forty-five inches. Its large rounded head lacks feather tufts, and it has dark brown, rather than yellow eyes.

Barred owls are quite common throughout the Finger Lakes Region though not in as great numbers as the great horned or the screech. Living in deep woods and along swamps, hiding by day in thick foliage, they are not often seen. However, being the most vocal of owls, they are often heard.

It's impossible to describe their variety of calls. One is a freakish bark. They also hoot but the call is more plaintive than that of the great horned. Most often it is a four syllable "Hoo-hoo-hoo-hoo." During courtship both partners "sing" a duet that is really something to hear. Owl fanciers call it "hooting it up."

Their nesting season is from April to May. They almost always nest in hollow trees. Because of their size they need large cavities in which to breed.

Nocturnal hunters, these owls often hunt over nearly open country in search of small mammals, frogs, snakes, lizards, mice, fish, and small birds.

Some ornithologists believe a few barred owls may turn into "snowbirds" because some years their numbers increase in southern areas during our winter.

Barn Owl (Monkey-faced Owl)

Slightly built and with long legs, barn owls appear somewhat ungainly. Because of their difference in structure they are classed in a separate family, *Tytonidae,* from all other owls which belong to the family *Strigidae.*

A barn owl is fourteen to twenty inches long and has a wingspan of forty to forty-five inches. It has a heart-shaped white face with black eyes. Its topside is tawny splashed with gray, white, and black. Underneath, it is white, and has small black dots on its breast.

True to their name, barn owls do live in barns. They are also found in silos, church towers, urban warehouses, graineries, and abandoned structures, places where there is an abundance of mice and rats. Farmers are happy to host barn owls because ninety percent of their diet is rodents. They also eat bats (caught in flight), squirrels, rabbits, beetles, crickets, grasshoppers, and small birds.

Barn owls just don't give a hoot. Instead they hiss like escaping steam, snap their beaks, and shriek maniacally. It's quite common for barn owls to set up housekeeping in abandoned houses, and may be the "ghosts" that are said to haunt some of them.

This owl's breeding habits are a bit irregular. Sometimes they raise one brood a year; sometimes two. In April, over a period of several days, the female lays five to seven — sometimes more — eggs on the floor of an upper story of a building. Like other owls' eggs, they are white. Incubation takes four to five weeks during which the male is the sole provider. The same pair of owls often uses the same site year after year.

23

The newly hatched owlets are covered with white down. In two weeks they have turned cream colored. By the time they are eight weeks old they have their adult plumage and are ready to fly.

A barn owl expresses anger and warning by dropping its head and swinging it to and fro while hissing loudly and snapping its beak.

Barn owls are non-migratory and nocturnal.

Flying Squirrels

Like many other nocturnal creatures that sleep by day, most of what has been learned about the lifestyle of the flying squirrel has come from observing captive specimens.

If you have been around the Finger Lakes for a while and still have not seen a flying squirrel, you are not alone. Recently a fellow I know, who had lived in the area all his life, turned on a light in his backyard and saw a small creature come gliding out of a tree and land on his bird feeder. For a moment he watched, puzzled. Suddenly he realized it had to be a flying squirrel about which he had only heard before. It was February 16th.

Measuring about nine inches from nose to tail tip, gray-brown in color, and with very large dark eyes, a flying squirrel's unique characteristic is a loose fur-covered membrane of skin called a patagium that stretches between its fore and hind legs on either side of its body. It does not actually fly. It cannot flap its patagium like wings and is unable to gain altitude while airborne.

Perhaps gliding squirrel would be a more accurate name. The squirrel leaps off a tree with all four legs horizontally extended, patagium pulled tight, and glides to a quiet, soft landing. Like a miniature hang-glider, it can volplane fifty yards or more. It can also, like other squirrels, travel on the ground. A flying squirrel's tail is not bushy like that of its larger cousin, the gray squirrel, but flat to serve as a rudder for braking.

There are lots of flying squirrels around. They aren't seen very much because people don't know they are there. There are two species in the Finger

Lakes region, nearly identical in appearance: the northern and the southern. The southern is slightly smaller, eats insects, fruits, tree buds, and nuts (mostly acorn and hickory). The northern varies its diet by adding lichens and fungi. Both occasionally dine on small birds, and both store up food for winter. The southern prefers a habitat of maple, beech, oak, and hickory, and is willing to live near humans, even in suburban attics. The northern will live in a mix of deciduous trees and conifers where it must contend with pugnacious red squirrels.

Clear cutting eliminates flying squirrels. They must have trees from which to launch.

Flying squirrels nest in abandoned woodpecker holes or natural tree cavities twenty to thirty feet above the ground; occasionally in outdoor nests like the gray squirrel's.

The northern mate from February to April and after a gestation of about forty days the female gives birth to two to four blind, naked babies from April to June. Their eyes open at about four weeks. They begin to experiment with glides at around seven weeks. In mid-summer they leave the nest. A devoted mother, the female crouches over her brood, patagium spread like a blanket. She carefully tends them until they are nearly full-grown. The southern generally mate a few weeks before.

If one of the babies falls from the nest, it emits a high-pitched cry, and the mother immediately glides to it, picks it up in her mouth and returns it to the nest.

During the winter, the squirrels— maybe a dozen or more— share a nest in a tree cavity, huddled together for warmth. Though not hibernators, they tend to remain in the nest during periods of extreme weather.

25

The best way to see flying squirrels, if you have trees with a bird feeder nearby, is to illuminate the feeder at night. The squirrels will soon get used to the light. If you turn off your indoor lights so your movements do not frighten them, you should soon see some of these interesting little creatures.

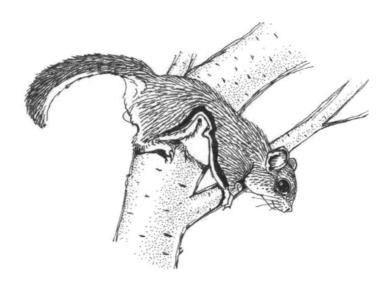

MARCH

Many people around the Finger Lakes consider March the most disagreeable month of the year, cold, blustery and drab. The snow is dirty and March winds are notoriously blustery. However, there also periods of warmth that make the fuzzy gray pussywillows burst out, and it is likely you will see your first robin of the season. Spring arrives late in the month, and usually the first peepers.

The Mourning Cloak

In March around the Finger Lakes, the cold wind blows and there is still some snow in patches on the ground. There is an occasional warm thaw too, enough to bring out the first butterfly on the wing in spring: the mourning cloak.

Moderately large, the mourning cloak measures up to three and a quarter inches from tip to tip of its spread wings. It is subject to some individual variation in color, but is usually dark brown with blue-edged wings

27

and spots with wide yellow or blue marginal bands, with submarginal rows of red mid-dorsal spots and several rows of spines the length of its body. It feeds on willow, poplar, hackberry, and rose leaves.

These butterflies spend the winter under leaves or in other sheltered places.

The Trilling of Peepers

In the Finger Lakes region, one of the most welcome sounds on an early spring evening is the trill of peepers. Almost as soon as the ice is out, usually after the temperature has reached about fifty degrees and stayed there for at least a few days, the tiny frogs called peepers come out of the mud where they have spent the winter, and start calling for mates. Every ditch, pool, pond, and marshy spot in the area echoes with their shrill trilling. Though the little creatures are no bigger than the end joint of your thumb, their voices can be heard for up to a mile. Close up in the quiet of an evening, the trilling of the multitude of the little amphibians can be deafening.

Most years, you first hear the peepers around the end of March. Only the males vocalize, usually while perched on vegetation near the water, or while partly sitting in it. They call for only a few weeks, and during that period their trilling may be somewhat sporadic. If the temperature falls below twenty degrees or so, they go back into the mud for a few days, and the countryside becomes quiet. When it warms up again, they emerge and resume their trilling. Country lore of the region says that peepers must be "frozen out" three times before warm weather will settle in for good.

28

When he is calling, a male peeper's throat puffs out into a pouch that is as big as he is, something like inflating a balloon. He has an actual larynx and vocal cords. He trills by passing air over his vocal cords.

Male peepers are darker green than the females; they have groins of yellow. Females can be distinguished quite easily by their white throats.

It takes a female peeper a day or more to lay her 800 to 1,300 cream and dark brown eggs, more or less separately, on supports under water such as cattails, stems of plants and weeds, and other vegetation. Once laid, she has no further interest in them. There is no parenting in the peeper family.

In five to fifteen days the eggs hatch. In seventy to ninety days the young have developed into one-and-one-half-inch tadpoles with purple-black blotches on their backs, and iridescent cream-colored bellies. By sometime in July the tadpoles have formed legs, lost their tails and become peepers. However, it will be three to four more years before they reach sexual maturity.

A peeper feeds on small insects it catches with a lightning-quick dart of its tongue. The little frog itself can become the victim of a snake, salamander, fish, bird, squirrel, or other predator.

During the summer, peepers sometimes are found quite far from water, even sixty feet up in trees.

Observing peepers calling is not as easy as you might think. Loud though they may be in leading you to their location, if they become aware of your presence, they will cease their trilling and slip back into the water out of sight. You must creep up on them slowly and quietly. If they suddenly become quiet, you should stop and wait a few minutes; they will start peeping again. Then, turn on your flashlight and stand in amazement at the wee size of the creature from which comes a voice of such volume!

Tree Frog Serenade

Tree frogs, also called tree toads, are close relatives of peepers and, like them, are part of the night symphony of the Finger Lakes area. You will also hear them during the day, especially if it is cloudy or rainy.

In the early spring, usually during March, the males head for marshy waterways and still ponds. In this environment they will sit and call for several nights. Finally, the females, lured by the serenade, quietly join them.

Like the peeper, the male tree frog has a bubble on his lower chin, which he inflates to produce his short melodic trill.

Male tree frogs measure about two inches; the females two and two thirds inches. The eggs—one female may lay 2,000 of them—hatch in four to five days into one quarter inch tadpoles, or polliwogs. They are gray, green or brown with red-orange tails and whitish bellies. It takes between forty-five and sixty-five days for the polliwogs to transform into frogs; another three years for the frogs to reach sexual maturity.

On most damp or rainy summer nights when the temperature is over sixty degrees, you will hear tree frogs trilling from the treetops. Often they are a considerable distance from water.

Tree frogs are not easy to find. They have "fingers," the ends of which are equipped with suction cups that enable them to cling to smooth surfaces. They can adjust their color to match their surroundings, going from gray to brown to green in a relatively short time. A green tree frog clinging to the underside of a leaf, or a brown one motionless in the mud can be pretty hard to spot.

Coyote (Prairie Wolf, Brush Wolf)

Smaller than a wolf but larger than a fox, a coyote looks a lot like a medium-sized shepherd dog. Coyotes are members of the dog family. However, its forelegs are heavier, its tail shorter and bushier, its coat thicker, its muzzle broader, and its nose more pointed. It is gray or reddish gray with rust-colored ears, legs, and feet and a whitish throat and belly. An identifying characteristic of the coyote is the way it holds its tail down between its hind legs when running, in contrast to a fox which holds its tail straight out.

Having pushed gradually eastward from the plains, there are a lot of coyotes in open woodlands and bushy areas around the Finger Lakes. Because they are primarily nocturnal, many people are unaware of their presence. A high-pitched yapping at night that increases in volume to a long yell or a quavering howl may be the first evidence that a family of coyotes is inhabiting an area.

A coyote is both a scavenger and hunter, eating mostly rodents and rabbits. If it ate only mice, it would consume ten thousand of them a year. Coyotes can detect small rodents underground by using their feet, even when there are several inches of snow. Worms, insects, and berries supplement its diet.

Coyotes have had a bad reputation as savage killers of domestic livestock. Sometimes when there is a shortage of their natural prey —rodents and rabbits —they do kill sheep, calves, and fawns. They are able to overcome these larger animals by attacking at the throat. Food is not wasted in the coyotc family. Whatever is not eaten immediately is cached for future consumption. Usually a burrow dug in a hill-

31

side, a cave or a hollow among rocks serves as a coyote's lair. The animals mate in January or February. After a sixty-three-day gestation, the female gives birth to a litter of about six pups in an immaculately kept nesting chamber. Brown all over and blind at birth, the pups' eyes open when they are nine days old. For the first six weeks they live on their mother's milk and on grasshoppers and crickets caught by their parents.

Coyotes mate for life. Just before the pups are born the male leaves the family den and takes up residence in a nearby burrow. He brings food to the family and, when the young are about two months old, takes them along on the hunt, joined by the female. They hunt as a family group until late summer when the young disperse. At two years of age they will choose mates.

The Eastern Cottontail

The eastern cottontail, so named because the underside of its abbreviated tail looks like a fluffy ball of cotton, is one of the most prolific animals of the Finger Lakes area, having four or five litters of from four to seven young each year during the warm months.

People joke a lot about the rabbits' fecundity. However, inasmuch as they are on the menu of predatory birds and animals and hunted by man, if they didn't multiply so rapidly they would be extinct in a short time.

The babies are born naked and blind, but by the second day they are covered with fur. At six to eight days they can see, hear, and crawl. At three to four weeks they leave the nest and disperse.

The mother rabbit, which has mated again soon after giving birth, starts work on a new nest, a shallow depression in the earth amongst weeds or under a brush pile. She lines it with leaves and grasses and fur she plucks from her belly, which she uses to cover the nest to protect it from excessive moisture. After a gestation period of from twenty-six-to-thirty days, the new brood is born.

An adult cottontail weighs two to three pounds. It is gray to reddish brown all year, and is common throughout the Finger Lakes area in brushy fields, open woods, public parks, edges of swamps, and in gardens. Around my place, the rabbits prefer to eat the clover that is abundant in my backyard. Mostly nocturnal feeders, rabbits eat mostly shoots and leaves. In winter, they feed on the bark of trees and shrubs. If they girdle trees or ornamentals, the plants die. With strong, chisel-like teeth, rabbits are gnawers. Understandably, orchard owners are not fond of them.

Some people call cottontails hares. However, rabbits and hares are different. A hare is larger and heavier than a rabbit, and has longer ears. Some hares turn white in winter; the cottontail stays the same color year-round. Jackrabbits and snowshoe rabbits are really hares.

In addition to natural predators, cottontails are hunted by man for their meat and fur. The cheaper grades of fur are used in the manufacture of felt hats and as linings for gloves and such. The better grades of fur, called cony, are used to make coats and trimmings.

The cottontail is well-equipped to detect danger. At the slightest sound its ears perk up and wave forward and backward to locate the source. It twitches its nostrils and moves its head up and down to catch the scent. Its large eyes, each of which sees more than 180°, are located on either side of its head. This enables them to observe a hawk overhead, while at the same time looking for brush to dash into.

A rabbit relies on speed to escape enemies. It can cover about eight feet in a bound, but doesn't have great endurance. The female rabbit or doe fights bravely in defense of her young or herself, by delivering a powerful kick or sometimes biting. The male rabbit or buck takes no part in family life.

Cottontails are solitary, each rabbit claiming a territory of two or three acres and knowing every inch of it intimately.

Rabbits have five toes on their forefeet; four on the hind. To bathe, it shakes each foot violently to get rid of dirt; then it licks it off. Like a cat, it washes its face with its front paws, but unlike a cat, it washes with both paws at the same time. The rabbit grooms its ears by pushing them forward with its hind feet to within reach of its tongue.

33

APRIL

According to the calendar, spring arrives in late March, but around the Finger Lakes, April is the month it finally appears. Wild shrubs begin to flower and the early spring wildflowers are in bloom. Pussywillows are out and the bass croak of the bullfrog reverberates through the evening air. Robins are back hopping about, pulling worms out of the ground. Sassafras trees are showing green, the tiger swallowtail butterfly is on the wing. There are showers, rainbows, and bluebirds.

Bursting Forth

From mid to late April, you will find small, bare-twigged trees and shrubs bursting forth with white puffs that look like popping corn. Known by several names, shadblow, shadberry, bilberry, serviceberry, serviceberry, its most common name, shadbush, is derived from its blooming period coinciding with the spawning migration of shad—a fish—up the rivers to the northeast. It is the region's earliest-flowering wild shrub. Its scientific name is *Amelanchier*.

There are about twenty-five sub-species of the plant, many closely related and difficult for the layman to distinguish. One of the loveliest, grandiflora, is easily recognized by its pinkish flowers. A natural hybrid of two other species, *laevis* and *canadensis*, it is particularly abundant in the Finger Lakes region.

As the drama of spring unfolds, the shadbush leaves unfurl and the petals fall from the branches. After a two-month intermission, the trees will be laden with small reddish-purple berry-like fruits, pulpy, sweet, edible, and delicious. They are the first wild fruits of the season, and eaten by a myriad of birds. From stomach records and observation, it has been found that at least thirty-six species of birds eat the berries. Some of the most common are robin, cedar waxwing, bluebird, cardinal, flicker, ruffed grouse, wild turkey, and quail.

The berries are good eaten right off the tree, the ten soft seeds scarcely noticeable. With the addition of a little lemon juice, they make delicious pies. The fruit also may be dried and substituted for raisins or currants.

The wood of the shadbush is very heavy; the fifth hardest of all our wood. If it grew large enough for lumbering, it would be more valuable than white oak for cabinet wood.

Amphibians Awaken — The Frogs

Relatives of toads and salamanders, frogs are amphibians with thin, smooth, moist, and clammy scale-less skins. They lay their eggs in shallow water in jelly-like masses. A small female can lay from two to three thousand eggs; a large one, six to eight thousand. Each egg is spherical, one-sixteenth inch in diameter, black above and a light cream-color below.

All frogs pass through a tadpole or polliwog stage. The teacup-sized batch of eggs swells to several times its original size before hatching into polliwogs with gills for breathing, tails for swimming, and horny beaks with which to nip off small bits of vegetation. At this stage the tadpoles are very much like fish.

In eight to ten weeks, depending on the temperature, the tadpole reaches a length of three to four inches. Its gills gradually disappear; its hind legs develop. A few days later it develops a right front leg soon followed by a left front leg. Its tail, like its gills, slowly disappears.

As it loses its gills, the polliwog swims to the edge of the pond and begins sniffing air into its lungs which grow larger as the gills are absorbed.

While growing, the tadpole has an intestine between two and three feet long that allows the animal to absorb enough nourishment from the large amounts of coarse vegetation it eats. Upon becoming a small frog, its intestine shortens to two inches, ample for a richer diet of insects, worms, and mosquitoes.

Temperature dictates the length of time it takes a tadpole to metamorphose into a frog. If the weather is warm it may take a week or less; if cool, two weeks or more.

Frogs spend their lives around water which they absorb through their skin and store in their bladders to keep their bodies moist. Frogs' moist skins contain a strong toxin. It will not hurt your hands but it is harmful if you get it in your mouth or rub it in your eyes. Therefore, if you handle these amphibians, wash your hands thoroughly as soon as possible.

A frog has a large mouth with wide gape-teeth on its upper jaw and in groups on the roof of its mouth. Its long tongue is attached at the front of its mouth and extends back into its throat. The frog flicks it out, catches its prey, and flips it back into its throat so fast the tongue is almost quicker than the eye. Sometimes it also uses its four-fingered "hands" to stuff struggling food into its mouth. They are also used to catch a branch toward which the frog has leaped, or to pull itself over an obstruction.

With large, powerful hindlegs, a frog can jump a long ways. Its five long webbed toes make swimming easy. To escape an enemy a frog dives headfirst into the water. If you don't see it first, the "plunk" can give you a start.

A frog's ears are smooth drumheads in back of its eyes; its voice is produced by air passing over vocal cords in the larynx. If caught by a snake, a frog actually screams. Snakes don't seem to be affected by the unpleasant alkaloid excreted by glands in the frog's skin. However, it causes dogs to drool.

During the winter a frog sleeps buried in the mud. Its second summer is spent eating and growing. Two to four weeks after ice-out in the third year, the males join other frogs in the shallow water at the edge of a pond or small lake in search of mates. Their low croaks attract the females. The latter are voiceless.

A frog is not full grown until it is about five years old. If it manages to avoid snakes, herons, fishes, muskrats, and other predators it may live twenty years or more.

Wood Frog

The wood frog appears in varying shades of brown to match the forest floor. It is easily identified by dark grey patches, similar to a robber's mask, that extend past each eye. Anywhere from one and one-half to three inches long, it is one of the earliest frogs to be seen in the spring. It spends the coldest months under a stone, log, or old stump.

The male wood frog's voice sounds a lot like the quack of a duck. and does not carry a great distance.

Pickerel Frog

Found in sphagnum bogs, cool clear water, and meadow streams, the pickerel frog is from one and three-quarters to three inches in length with squarish, dark green spots. The concealed surfaces of its hind legs are bright yellow. Vocalizing males sound as if they are snoring.

Leopard Frog

Two to three and one-half inches, the leopard frog can be distinguished from the pickerel frog by its irregular rows of rounded black spots with dark cream colored borders all over its back and legs. As in all frogs, its underside is cream in color. Gathering two to three weeks after the ice has melted, they breed from March to May, and can be located by the low croaks of the males.

Leopard frogs have skin gland secretions that snakes find distasteful.

38

Green Frog

Green frogs are abundant throughout the Finger Lakes area. Two and one-fourth to three and one-half inches, they can be found around springs, creeks, ditches and the edges of ponds and lakes. The adult male has a yellow throat.

Breeding season for green frogs lasts from April to August. If you hear what sounds like the plucked string of a bass viol, it is probably a green frog.

Bull Frog

With a broad head and a body measuring up to eight inches long, and legs up to ten inches long, the bullfrog is the largest frog around the Finger Lakes. The southern bullfrog, is the biggest frog in America.

The appetite of a bullfrog matches its size. Its long sticky tongue is attached at the front of its mouth and extends back into the throat. It flips out to catch prey with lightning speed and precision. Its teeth are on the upper jaw only and in two small groups on the roof of its mouth. Besides insects, it feeds on small fish, baby turtles, salamanders, small birds, crayfish, and small snakes. It also eats tadpoles and smaller frogs.

In turn, bullfrogs are eaten by large snakes, fish, ducks, crows, snapping turtles, hawks, herons, and other water birds. Additionally,

39

frog legs appear on the menus of many upscale restaurants. Frogs have long been used for experimental purposes in biological laboratories. In recent years frog populations have dwindled alarmingly. In some areas laws have been passed making it illegal to catch frogs for market during their April—May breeding season. Most of the frogs sold in the market today are commercially raised in "frog farms."

A frog's arms are small with four fingers on each hand. It has five long, webbed toes on each foot and can hop, dive, and swim.

Greenish, with a net-like pattern of gray or brown and a skin ridge over each eye, a bullfrog has legs so powerful it can leap ten times its length. The record in a frog jumping contest held annually is sixteen feet four inches for three jumps one after another, held by a six-inch bullfrog.

A bullfrog is an amphibian, spending its life in the water, in ponds, small lakes, and slow-moving streams. In winter, it buries itself in the soft mud at the bottom and goes to sleep.

In spring, bullfrogs come out of hibernation to find mates. That's when you hear the male's vibrant bass "chug-a-rum." A bullfrog sings with its mouth shut, drawing in air through his nose. Voice sacs at his throat cause the skin to balloon out as the singing begins. His voice can carry for up to one-half of a mile. The female may sing, but not loud or often. Her voice sacs do not balloon out.

The female bullfrog lays up to 20,000 eggs in a jelly-like mass in shallow water among the weeds. Each egg is about one-sixteenth-inch in diameter. The time it takes the eggs to hatch into tadpoles and then develop into frogs depends on the water temperature. It takes longer if the water is cold. It may take two or three years for a bullfrog egg to become a frog. It is full-grown at about five years. There is no parenting in the bullfrog family. Naturalists think a bullfrog can live for up to thirty years.

The American Toad

Many people confuse frogs and toads. Though they are related, there are significant differences. A frog has smooth moist skin, while a toad has thick, dry, rough, and warty skin. Both are amphibians but frogs spend most of their lives in or near water while toads live on land. Frogs have long legs and are great jumpers. With shorter legs, toads jump only when frightened.

Unlike frogs, toads have no teeth. Mostly they just sit, eat, and grow. Flipping out its sticky tongue and catching insects, a toad fills its stomach four times in twenty-four hours. One year I had a resident toad in my garden all summer. Invariably, I would find it hunched into a shallow depression that was shaded by squash leaves. It seemed to be there almost all the time, and it got fatter and fatter.

As in a frog, a toad's tongue is attached at the front of its mouth. Most of its food —mosquitoes, crickets, cutworms, flies, beetles, and slugs —is caught with its tongue. It also relishes earthworms, but it must gradually work one into its mouth with its forefeet before swallowing it whole.

When frightened, a toad puffs out its body until its skin becomes taut. If handled roughly it oozes a milky, acrid secretion, harmless to humans unless it reaches the eyes or mouth. It is just a superstition that you can get warts by handling toads.

Toads hibernate under clods of earth, logs, or stones. In the spring the males join other amphibians in a pool and begin calling to the females. The male has a vocal sac under his chin that swells up into a balloon larger than his head as air is driven back and forth between lungs

41

and mouth. His song is a long trill.

A few days after mating, the female lays thousands of small black eggs in shallow water; they are strung like a double strand of beads. From two to three days up to a week, depending on the temperature, the eggs hatch into tiny tadpoles, much smaller and darker than frog tadpoles. Only a small percentage will reach maturity, the majority falling prey to fish, herons, turtles, crayfish, and other creatures.

Those that survive will be about an inch long in four to six weeks. In a few more days they will have turned into toads which have shrunk to about the size of your little fingernail. They leave the water, hiding by day from their terrestrial enemies: snakes, hawks, crows, and domestic fowl. At night they migrate even farther from their home pool, feeding on mosquitoes and other small insects. By the time they are ready hibernate in the fall they are again about an inch long.

At about three years of age, like the frog, a male toad makes his first pilgrimage to a pool to mate.

A full grown toad may be three and one-half inches long and can live to be about twenty-five years old.

A Colorful World

Of all the things in nature that delight the eye, wildflowers are among the most appreciated. It's a real thrill to discover a species you haven't seen before, or to finally find a rare species for which you have been searching.

There are about a thousand species of wildflowers in the Finger Lakes area. They bloom from March to November in habitats varying from the roadsides to remote bogs. They are not always easy to identify. Some species appear in more than one color. For example, hepaticas can be blue, pink, or white. Teasels are usually lavender, but along the Southern Tier Expressway south of Elmira and beside Route 31 near Montezuma, you can see white ones. Also, flowers may be different in size in different habitats. Particularly confusing are flowers that have hybridized, which is quite common. I think I've seen a dozen hybrid violets. Not to worry. Even trained botanists often have trouble identifying hybrid species.

Some of our wildflowers are native to the Finger Lakes; others have been introduced and are said to be "alien." Many are from Europe: Queen Anne's Lace (wild carrot), chicory, dandelion, teasel, butter and eggs, bouncing bet, spearmint, peppermint, red clover, white clover, and mullein, among others.

Some plants, sundews and pitcher plants for instance, live in such wet, nutrient-poor environments that they supplement their energy needs by trapping and digesting insects. They attract insects by exhibiting a sweet smell or glistening fluid that suggests nectar, but acts to trap their prey for digestion.

A wildflower is said to belong to a "family": heath family, snapdragon family, mint family (square-stemmed), primrose family, even the tomato (nightshade) family.

After the long Finger Lakes winter, early spring wildflowers are a most welcome sight. However, to find them you usually have to leave the beaten path and venture into the woods, swamps, and bogs. You can see the most variety with the least effort during August on a ride through the countryside.

At any time during the growing season you will find the most species, many rare, in the Mundy Wildflower Garden at the Cornell Plantations. The information center lists those currently in bloom, and there are color-coded markers for identification. Located in an eight-acre

43

glacially created flood plain of Fall Creek, the garden has well-maintained gravel paths for easy walking. In addition to flowers you will see many different trees and shrubs.

You should never pick wildflowers. Like many other things in nature, their habitat is shrinking. Some, such as trilliums, grow from bulbs which are nourished by the plant's dying leaves. Picking them destroys the plants. Picking a protected species is against the law.

An extremely rare plant, Leedy's roseroot, prevalent during the Ice Age but now known to occur in only five sites in the world, grows on a cliff on the west shore of Seneca Lake. Its location is secret and is protected by an easement held by the Nature Conservancy.

Arcs in the Sky

You probably learned the colors of the rainbow when you were in elementary school: red, orange, yellow, blue, green, and violet. Down through the ages peoples have looked at rainbows in many different ways. In early times they were mystified by rainbows and invented fables to explain the colorful arc in the sky.

Perhaps because the rainbow usually appears at the end of a storm, the ancient Hebrews interpreted it as a symbol of God's promise never again to destroy the earth by flood. The Norsemen perceived the rainbow as a bridge between their home in the sky and the earth. In Greek mythology, Iris was a rainbow goddess who, they believed, carried messages from the gods down to men on the earth via the rainbow. The Greeks also saw it as a sign placed in the heavens by the gods to foretell war or heavy rain.

Then, in 1666, Sir Isaac Newton discovered the scientific answer to the mystery of the rainbow. While trying to learn what caused the color fringes in telescope lenses, he passed a beam of light through a prism, and found that white light is a mixture of colored lights, and that each color is bent by a different amount when it passes through a prism. To make a rainbow, raindrops act together as a giant prism. Light comes from the drops which are curved, hence the bow.

Rainbows vary in intensity of color and in their duration. A primary (single) rainbow has red on its outside edge; a secondary (double) one has red on its inside edge.

Most rainbows occur late in the day when the sun begins to shine soon after a rain, but while the air is still filled with raindrops. You most often see one when the sun is at your back while the rain is still falling in the distance ahead of you.

Though we usually think of rainbows as being in the sky, you can also see one in the spray of a waterfall, a lawn sprinkler, in the wake of a motorboat. These rainbows are, of course, much smaller and usually less colorful than a solar rainbow.

Screech Owl

Most breeding adult screech owls settle within a mile from where they were raised. For the screech owls of the Finger Lakes, egg laying begins about the first of April in a tree cavity or in the abandoned nest of another bird. The usual clutch is four round, white eggs. During the twenty-five to thirty day incubation period, the female is totally dependent on her lifelong mate for food, which he deposits directly into the nest cavity. The female leaves the nest only briefly once a day to drink and to defecate.

After about twenty-seven days, the owlets fledge in the order they were hatched, usually one or two per night. Newly hatched screech owls have a scanty coat of white down, gradually replaced with thicker gray or

45

red down. The colors have nothing to do with age, sex or the season. Owlets of both colors may share the same nest and have the same parents.

Screech owls are seven to ten inches tall with a wingspan of eighteen to twenty-four inches, and weigh six to eight ounces. On average, the males weigh seventeen percent less than the females. Their average lifespan is about three and one-half years.

These owls are nocturnal, usually discovered by their quavering, tremulous, descending trill. They nest in orchards, parks, and suburbs where the lots are wooded. They make good— though sometimes noisy—neighbors. No other owl around the Finger Lakes consumes such a wide variety of pest insects. Rodents, small fish, crustaceans, earthworms, small snakes, and birds supplement their diets.

Cold Blooded Residents — the Snakes

Contrary to popular opinion, snakes are not slimy. Their long slender bodies are covered with transparent, dry, overlapping scales. They have up to 400 vertebrae (humans have thirty-three). Their ribs are not attached to their breastbones, allowing them to expand when swallowing a large meal. Actually, snakes "walk" on their ribs.

They are all meat eaters, consuming fish, birds, insects, eggs, small mammals, earthworms, amphibians, and other snakes. They swallow their prey whole and alive, with the exception of poisonous snakes which kill their prey before eating.

The large size of the prey a snake can swallow is remarkable. Its upper and lower jaws are joined by hinge-like bones that allow its mouth to open extremely wide. Each side of its jaws can move independently so the snake can maneuver its mouth around large prey. Sharp teeth that slant backward prevent prey from escaping. It can take up to an hour for it to swallow a sizeable victim. If you see a snake with a big bulge in its body it has just consumed a meal. It may not eat again for several days.

As a snake grows it sheds its skin. When molting is imminent its eye scales become cloudy and its vision is impaired. It takes some time to wriggle out of the old skin and the effort tires the animal. However, when finished the snake's lidless eyes are once again clear under a transparent covering and its colors are shiny. Non-poisonous snakes have round eye pupils while poisonous snakes have a vertical pupil.

A snake's most vital sense organ is its long, forked tongue. As it flicks it out it picks up scent particles from the air and the ground. Then it sticks its tongue into a cavity inside its head called Jacobson's organ which is lined with sensory cells. All snakes lack external ears.

Cold-blooded, like all reptiles, a snake's body is controlled by the temperature of their environment. A snake will seek cover from intense midday heat, but when it is cool it will bask in the sun. Cold temperatures make snakes sluggish.

During the winter snakes hibernate, sometimes alone, but more often in groups in dens. Upon emerging in the spring they slowly return to life. As soon as they are back to normal they are ready to mate. Like many animals they find mates by smell. As they twine their two bodies together the male's sperm cells pass into the female's body. After mating they live separately during spring and summer.

Some species of snakes give birth to live young; others (called eggers) lay eggs. Either may produce from two to one hundred young. The eggers lay their eggs in piles of rotting wood or leaves about a month after mating. They are long, narrow and flexible, resembling a big medicine-like capsule. The shells are tough and leathery. They are left to develop on their own. An egger baby has a special tooth on its upper jaw to cut through the shell which falls out soon after hatching.

Live birth snake babies come into the world in August or September individually encased in transparent membranes which they quickly break. Right from birth they are on their own.

Snakes have unequalled agility. They can swim, climb tree trunks, and

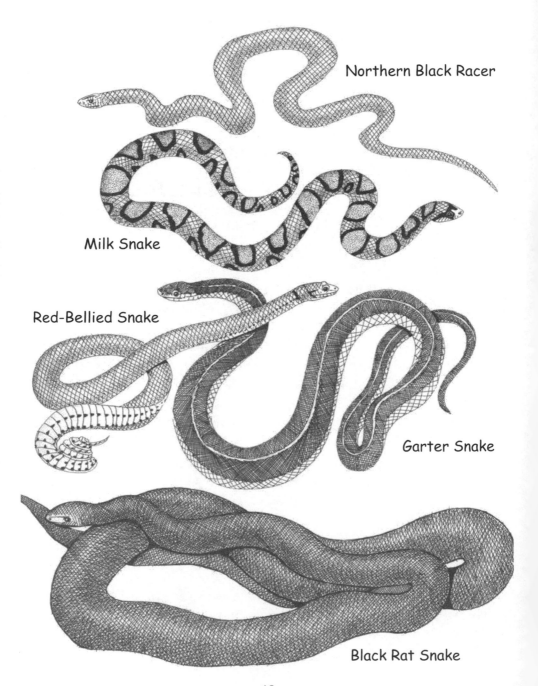

Northern Black Racer

Milk Snake

Red-Bellied Snake

Garter Snake

Black Rat Snake

48

cover distances on the ground with amazing speed. However, they cannot travel well on a very smooth surface, such as glass.

Eagles, hawks and owls prey on snakes, but their biggest predator by far is man.

There are eighteen known species of snakes in New York State. The following are some of the more common you are likely to find around the Finger Lakes.

Garter Snake

The garter snake is the snake you will encounter most often around the Finger Lakes. Without venom, it is harmless to humans though, like any snake, it will bite if cornered. Though not poisonous, its bite may cause infection, so you should seek medical attention if you are bitten. It's more likely the snake will exude an extremely foul odor to keep you at bay.

There is but one species of the common garter snake but it includes several subspecies, therefore, all garter snakes do not look alike. Usually they have yellow stripes but some have green or brown stripes or some no stripes at all. Most are small, slim-bodied and seldom exceed thirty inches in length. They exist mostly on a diet of insects, mice, frogs, salamanders, and earthworms, and are found in fields, woods, marshes, ditches, and other damp places where such food is abundant.

The female garter snake gives birth to between twenty-five and seventy-five live young per season. They are born from June to August, and mature in two years. The oldest known garter snake lived to be ten years old.

Garter snakes often hibernate in great numbers. One April, I stumbled onto one of their denning areas on a rocky bank on the east side of Seneca Lake a few miles north of Watkins Glen. There was a huge ball of them twisting and writhing together while many more were slithering around the ball. There must have been hundreds of them.

Milk Snake

A milk snake is a fairly large reptile, often reaching over forty inches in length. Light gray with coppery-brown spots, each ringed with black, it has a black and white irregular checkerboard belly.

Harmless to humans, milk snakes prey mostly on mice which make up seventy percent of their diet. They are secretive and are inclined to stay around barns where rodents are plentiful. Apparently this tendency gave rise to the old but untrue idea that they sucked milk from cows.

Milk snakes are egg layers.

Water Snake

The water snake is a fairly large, heavy-bodied reptile that is found, as its name implies, in and around water. Because it tends to be more aggressive than other snakes around the Finger Lakes some people think it is poisonous. They are probably confusing it with the southern cottonmouth or water moccasin which is also a water snake, and is venomous. However, the cottonmouth extends up the east coast only as far north as the Dismal Swamp area of Virginia.

You often find water snakes sunning on a beaver lodge or on a rock or branch beside a pond, lake, or stream. They usually swim with their heads above water. They sometimes congregate around old dug wells, and it's not uncommon for them to set up housekeeping among the timbers of lakeside docks. Cottage owners around the Finger Lakes find them persistent tenants.

Water snakes do not like to be disturbed. They may move off very slowly or hold their own. If pressed, they can show remarkably disagreeable dispositions, and can be quite intimidating. Sometimes it's hard to believe they haven't the venom to back up their belligerence.

One identifying feature of a water snake is the dark grey markings that are larger than the spaces between them.

Northern Black Racer

The northern black racer is a slender, fast moving snake of which you may get only a glimpse as it streaks away. It often retreats upward into bushes or low branches of trees. However, if it is cornered it puts up a fierce fight.

Uniformly black both above and below, the black racer usually has some white on its chin and throat. Baby racers are patterned with gray or reddish brown.

Thirty-six to sixty inches long and diurnal, the black racer subsists on a diet of rodents, frogs, insects, lizards, small birds, and other snakes. It is an egger, the eggs of which are coated with small lumps that look like coarse grains of salt.

Black Rat Snake

The black rat snake is the largest non-poisonous reptile in the Finger Lakes area. It is heavy bodied and measures from forty-two to seventy-two inches long. The largest on record measured 101 inches. It is plain, shiny black with a whitish belly with indistinct checker-boarding. After a heavy meal, when its body is distended, it shows a fainter spotted pattern. Unlike the adults, the babies are boldly patterned.

The rocky, forested hillsides of the Finger Lakes are ideal habitat for the black rat snake. It is a superb climber and sometimes takes up residence in a cavity high up in a hollow tree. Its diet consists of young rats, mice, birds, lizards, small mammals, and frogs. It is especially fond of tree frogs. To capture prey it lunges forward, body reared upward and quickly wraps itself around its victim.

The black rat snake is a constrictor. It has a ferocious hiss. When frightened the snake vibrates its tail rapidly, which produces a sound similar to a rattlesnake, especially in dry leaves.

Northern Ringneck Snake

Slender and only ten to fifteen inches long, the northern ringneck is hardly a threat to anyone. It's a secretive little woodland reptile that hides in logs, slabs of bark, rotting wood, or under stones.

It's one of the easiest snakes to identify, brownish-grey and unpatterned except for a gold band around its neck. Its belly is gold as well and a gold tail that appears twisted due to coloration.

Like the black rat snake, the northern ringneck likes the rocky, wooded hillsides of the Finger Lakes. It feeds mostly on earthworms, small salamanders, lizards, frogs, and insects.

Eastern Smooth Green Snake

Though the Eastern smooth green snake is common around the Finger Lakes, sightings of it are not. It is shy and retiring and its protective coloration is so perfect you can look right at it and not see it unless it moves. It is not large, seldom exceeding twenty inches in length.

Grassy fields, moist sphagnum bogs and, particularly, sheltered glens are the preferred habitat of these reptiles. It's possible, however, to see one in your garden. They eat mostly crickets, spiders, smooth caterpillars, and grasshoppers.

Unlike other snakes, the smooth green is uniformly smooth because its scales lack the longitudinal ridges which divide the dorsal scales of many common snakes, such as the garter. The feel of the smooth green's skin has been described as resembling fine suede.

Non-venomous, one of these snakes is completely at the mercy of its captor. However, when grasped, it whips its body about wildly usually startling its assailant into dropping it so it can escape.

Northern Brown Snake (Formerly DeKay's Snake)

Measuring nine to thirteen inches, the northern brown snake is often mistaken for a small garter snake. It can be light yellowish brown, gray to dark brown or a deep reddish brown, with two rows of blackish spots down its back. Its belly is light-colored. Its territory is widespread and it can be found in marshes, moist woods, bogs, and on hillsides, parks, and cemeteries throughout the Finger Lakes.

It is, however, an expert when it comes to hiding. In an effort to be less conspicuous, the northern brown snake flattens its body when alarmed. Like the garter snake, it releases a foul odor from its anal scent glands if it is picked up.

Slugs, earthworms, and soft-bodied insects make up most of the reptile's diet.

The northern brown snake was originally named "DeKay's Snake" after James Edward DeKay, an early New York naturalist.

Red-bellied Snake

The red-bellied snake is not common around the Finger Lakes, but can sometimes be seen in upland open woods and in or near spaghnum bogs in the region. Even if you're not fond of snakes it's exciting to see one of these rare, secretive little creatures.

The red-bellied is subject to color variation. Usually they are plain brown, but some are gray and a minority are black. Their bellies vary too from bright red to orange to yellow. They have three pale spots at the nape of their necks.

A Note About Poisonous Snakes...

It's unlikely you will encounter a poisonous snake around the Finger Lakes region. Harry Greene of the Department of Ecology at Cornell University says they are "few and far between." There are no copperheads at all. However, there are two colonies of timber rattlesnakes along the Chemung River west of Elmira and a few in Steuben County. One or two people have reported seeing timber rattlers just south of Ithaca, but they haven't provided either a specimen or a photo for identification.

A smaller rattler, the Massasauga, can be found in a small area north of Syracuse and in Bergen Swamp near Rochester.

Sassafras

In early April the countryside around the Finger Lakes is pretty drab. The chartreuse blossoms of the sassafras tree are often the first real green of spring. The blooms soon fall and are replaced by leaves of the same chartreuse color which darken into a rich green.

The leaves may be the most interesting part of the sassafras tree. Some look like mittens with the thumb on the right or the left. Some have no lobes at all. All the variations may occur on the same tree.

In August, blue-green seeds about the size of pea beans top clusters of red stems. In autumn the leaves turn an orange-red.

The aromatic sassafras is an American native, a member of the laurel family, growing all around the Finger Lakes. The native Americans taught the newly arrived Europeans to use the bark and the roots to make tea and mouthwash.

In 1586, Sir Francis Drake took sassafras roots

from America to Europe. The tea made from them quickly became the rage in England. However, eventually word spread that sassafras was used by the Indians in America to cure syphilis. Soon, no one would be seen drinking the tea in public.

Years ago, sassafras was the flavoring used in homemade root beer. Now it is used as a fragrance in medicines, soaps, cleansers, and brewed as herbal tea.

On the Wing

Usually on the wing in early April, the tiger swallowtail is the largest yellow butterfly around the Finger Lakes, measuring four to six and one-half inches. Though typically creatures of woodlands and meadows, they are found in city gardens and around mud puddles, manure, and carrion. They are easy to catch as they busily sip the nectar of the flower on which they perch. Unfortunately, like all butterflies, their wings are so fragile the slightest touch damages them for life.

Tiger swallowtail larvae live in a one-leaf nest it folds over itself, often high up in trees. It feeds on wild cherry, tulip trees, birch, poplar, ash, and basswood. The insect hibernates as a pupa; rough, brown in its larval stage and green mottled.

55

New York's Official Bird

A hundred years ago bluebirds were as common as robins around the Finger Lakes, and everyone loved them. In fact, the Eastern bluebird was named the official bird of New York State. However, their numbers began to dwindle as old orchards and hedgerows, their chief nesting sites, were bulldozed to make bigger farms and vineyards.

Then came the insecticide DDT. It killed the insects, and because bluebirds are largely insect eaters it also killed many of them. Those that survived were unable to raise young because the DDT caused their eggs to have soft shells. Eventually the full scope of the residual effects of DDT became known and it was banned, but not before it had greatly diminished the bluebird population in the area.

Bluebird lovers got busy and put up nesting boxes for the remaining birds and eventually their numbers increased. Now they are quite common here though the bluebird is still on New York State's "special concern" list.

I believe most bluebirds now raise their families—two to three broods a year—in backyard nesting boxes. Bird clubs also have established "bluebird trails," a series of boxes at least 100 yards apart along a path a mile or so in length.

It is easy to become protective of a family of bluebirds which have taken up residence in your backyard. They are sweet and timid, so when a horde of tree swallows tries to take over the nesting box you might find yourself helping the bluebirds fend off the more aggressive swallows.

The female bluebird is the architect, contractor, and builder of the nest. Construction takes about three days during which she carries bunch after bunch of dry grasses into the nest. While building, however, she expects her mate to provide sustenance. Periodically she flies to a branch, flutters her wings and chirps noisily. The male wastes no time in picking up morsels from the ground and feeding them to her.

Egg laying begins when the nest is complete. Four to five in number, the eggs are pale blue and smaller then a robin's. You rarely see the female while she is nesting. The male is always close by, perched where he can see the nest. Several times a day he takes food to the nest.

It takes about thirty-eight days for egg laying, incubation, and fledging. When the babies fledge, they waste no time leaving the nest and generally stay with the family only about two more weeks. The young are duller in color than their parents with mottled breasts.

Bluebirds are migratory but some individual birds do remain throughout the winter.

If you want to attract bluebirds to your backyard, build or buy a nesting box made especially for them. They are picky house hunters — just any old birdhouse won't work.

MAY

Birdsong fills the warm days of May in the Finger Lakes region. Ruby-throated hummingbirds arrive at feeders; the black swallowtail butterfly wafts gracefully on the soft spring breezes. Female turtles lumber out of the muddy pond bottoms where they have spent the winter and look for a place to lay their eggs. Wildflowers are at their peak and the deciduous trees are putting on their cloaks of green; new animal babies arrive daily. There is a plethora of newly-hatched insects, and hungry snakes to gobble them up. And bullheads are biting!

Roman Goddess

The Luna Moth, named for the Roman Goddess, is one of the most exquisite of all flying creatures. It is an unusual pale green color with graceful, curved, trailing hind wings bejeweled with transparent eyespots ringed with pale yellow, blue, and black. Its forewings are edged with lavender; its feathery antennae are straw-colored. Because it drifts silently through the night it is rarely seen, but when it is, it is seldom forgotten.

As an adult the Luna lives but a few days. For the female those days are stressful. She mates and after her nuptial flight her breathtaking beauty is gone. Her fragile wings are torn and broken; she looks utterly bedraggled. Before she dies, however, she will summon enough energy to lay her bun-shaped, shiny blue-green eggs singly or in masses on leaves of a host plant. In the Finger Lakes area this is usually in a hickory or walnut tree.

It takes seven or eight days for the tiny, dark-green larva to emerge. The female Luna eats continuously, pausing only for each of its eight molts. When full grown, the caterpillar measures upwards of three inches. It is pea green, fat, with narrow white stripes and red dots. Feeding upside-down on a twig, it is quite well concealed.

In about a month the caterpillar's voracious appetite begins to taper off. Finally it ceases eating altogether and empties its digestive tract, which causes it to become smaller. It is now ready to pupate. It takes twenty-four hours for the caterpillar to fashion its cradle-shaped cocoon. With thread from silk organs in its head, it stitches together leaves which it reinforces with leafy particles. In this casing it spins the silken cocoon in which it will spend the winter.

The adult Luna emerges in May.

The Life of the Muskrat

You'll find muskrats in ponds and marshes, and along rivers and lakes — anywhere there is thick vegetation for both food and cover. You most often see their houses in open swamps though they are also found along the edges of ponds and rivers; even in roadside ditches where there is a substantial flow of water.

A muskrat house looks like a large pile of water vegetation. It is usually constructed with branches, cattails, and other water plants to about four feet high and five feet across. The walls of a muskrat house are cemented with mud. Inside, above the water mark, is the nest made of finely shredded leaves. It has several tunnels that connect it to underground exits. These are either camouflaged by piles of vegetation or built below the level of the thickest ice in winter. Breathing holes are kept open by constantly breaking the ice as it forms.

Muskrats serve a useful purpose in keeping waterways open by eating vegetation. However, their tunneling also breaches banks of streams and pond dikes causing considerable damage. Farmers usually try to keep them out of their farm ponds.

A muskrat is a large vole, twelve or so inches in length with a scaly, almost hairless flattened tail seven to eleven inches long which serves as a rudder when the rodent is swimming. Partly webbed hind feet enhance its agility in the water.

A muskrat can remain submerged under water for up to twelve minutes. In winter it digs roots out of the muddy bottom. Its main diet consists of these roots, leaves of water plants (cattails, arrowhead, lilies, wild rice), crayfish, mussels, and rarely, fish.

60

Muskrats are prolific, raising several families during the spring and summer months. After a gestation period of about twenty-six days the female gives birth to from five to seven young. The two to three inch babies are naked, blind, and helpless. At one month, however, they are weaned and driven out of the nest by their mother who has mated right after their birth and will soon have another litter to care for.

Muskrats face many dangers: floods, great horned owls, red-tailed hawks, foxes, raccoons, coyotes, snapping turtles, pike, and water snakes. By far their most dangerous predator is the mink. Naturally, the young are the most vulnerable.

The muskrat gets its name from the musky-smelling secretions of two glands on the base of its tail. Ranging in color from silvery brown to almost black, its rich fur, with a layer of short downy hairs under its long, coarse guard-hairs, is very valuable. The meat is said to be tasty too. In the United States it is marketed in gourmet shops as "marsh rabbit" or "Chesapeake terrapin."

If you see a muskrat away from water, it is most likely searching for new breeding grounds.

The Turtles

A turtle is a compactly built reptile known for its protective shell, the carapace, an arched bony growth usually made up of plates that covers its back. Protecting its underside is the plastron, which is formed by clavicles and abdominal bones. In almost all turtles the two are joined in such a way as to leave openings through which the head and legs can be retracted under the shell. Thus protected, a turtle is safe unless it gets flipped over on its back. It cannot right itself. When threatened they hiss like a snake.

A turtle's limbs usually end in five toes. Fresh water turtles like those around the Finger Lakes have rowing legs partially flattened laterally. The digits are distinct but joined by webbed membranes.

With a beak-like mouth, a turtle cuts off pieces of food and swallows them whole. There are no teeth on its jawbone, just sharp horny edges.

As a rule the male turtle's tail is longer than the female's. Both have small but well developed brains and thick moveable eyelids. All turtles reproduce by laying eggs, two to twenty to the clutch. Cold-blooded vertebrates, they rely on the sun to bring their bodies up to a functioning temperature. During the winter turtles hibernate burrowed under the soft muck at the bottom of ponds and slow streams.

Painted Turtle

You will find the painted turtle where the water is shallow and sluggish, choked with aquatic vegetation, and covered with a green mat of algae: ponds, marshes, backwaters, and ditches with soft muddy bottoms.

Four-to-seven-inches long, these reptiles have smooth shells patterned with red, yellow, and olive or black. Margins of the shell are red and black. The plastron is yellow and may have an irregular greenish-grey spot in the center. Two bright yellow spots on each side of the head are very distinct. The females are larger than the males which, when adult, have very long nails on their forefeet. Baby painted turtles usually measure one inch or less in length.

Like most turtles, the painted eat a huge amount of aquatic vegetation,

supplementing their diets with insects, crayfish, and small mollusks. They winter in as much as eighteen inches of muck.

There are fourteen subspecies of painted turtles. They are baskers, easily seen if you are in their habitat. You see a lot of them in the Montezuma National Wildlife Refuge.

Mud Turtle

Mud turtles are found in sluggish streams, small pools, or in roadside ditches where there are lots of water plants and a food supply of snails, worms, tadpoles, and water insects. The little reptiles crawl along the bottom, occasionally climbing out to sun themselves on a bank or tree stump.

With a shell length of but four inches and mud brown coloring, they often go unnoticed. The males have larger heads and longer tails than the females. They also have plates of horny scales on their hind legs which they use to clasp the female during mating. Mud turtle courtship occurs in the water. The male comes up behind the female and gives her a nudge. For a time they swim side by side. When the female stops it is a signal for the male to climb onto her back.

The female lays up to seven eggs in a nest under rotten logs or dug in the earth. The young hatch out in sixty to ninety days, depending on how warm the temperature is, and are approximately one inch long.

Male mud turtles mature in four to seven years; the females in five to eight. In captivity they have been known to live forty years. However, in the wild they can fall prey to crows, raccoons, and king snakes. If a skunk finds a turtle nest it will eat the eggs.

Stinkpot Turtle

Aptly named for the musky odor it emits when threatened, this small turtle is the only musk turtle north of Dixie. Three to five inches, it has a smooth carapace that varies in color from light greenish-brown to almost black, and is sometimes spotted and streaked. The female has a very small tail; the male a blunt and horny one. Slender appendages are visible on the chins and throats of both sexes.

If you see what looks like a stone patrolling the bottom of a clear water lake or pond it is probably a stinkpot. They are abundant throughout the Finger Lakes area, especially in still waters.

Stinkpots often climb six feet or more up branches of shrubs and trees at the water's edge.

Wood Turtle

Wood turtles are at home in water. However, they are the most terrestrial of all turtles around the Finger Lakes, wandering through meadows, farmlands, vineyards, woods and, unfortunately, roads.

Five to seven inches in length, this rare turtle is identified by its very rough grey-green shell and orange on its neck and limbs.

Spotted Turtle

You can't miss the spotted turtle. Three and one-half to four and one-half inches long, its grey carapace is sprinkled with yellow spots, the number of which varies widely from turtle to turtle.

Like most other turtles, it prefers a watery habitat: ponds, bogs, marshy meadows, and swamps where it is seen basking on a log or a stone.

Naturalists don't know why, but spotted turtles are seen much more often in the spring than during summer or fall.

Snapping Turtle

Of the seven species of turtles around the Finger Lakes the snapper is the largest. It can attain a length of three feet from its nose to the tip of its tail and weigh more than thirty-five pounds. Snappers are common, but because they spend most of their time in the water they are seen less often than some other species. Also, they rarely bask in the sun like most other turtles.

A female snapper begins egg laying when she has reached a weight of about three pounds, or about fifteen years of age. Egg-laying occurs in early June. It is the only time the female leaves the water, and the time of most frequent sightings as she crawls from the water and lumbers over land in search of a suitable place to lay her eggs. The nest must be where it will not

65

flood and where the temperature will be within certain limits. Often it is in a cultivated field or a pond dike. She may travel several hundred feet, even crossing a highway. This is very hazardous for the slow moving turtle.

Once the site is chosen, using her hind feet, the female digs a hole in the soft earth six to twelve inches deep into which she lays about ten to thirty spherical, leathery-shelled white eggs about an inch in diameter. She covers them with dirt and packs it down. She then returns to the water, leaving the eggs in the hands of fate. Many do not make it to hatching. They are a delicacy savored particularly by rats, frogs, snakes, skunks, raccoons, ducks, night herons, and other water birds. Only about two in twenty survive.

In about two and a half months baby snappers poke their noses up out of the moist soil and slowly inch their half-dollar sized bodies up into the daylight world. They immediately head for water where many of them are gobbled up by muskrat, largemouth bass, and other fish. Late-hatched snappers overwinter in the nest.

Active mainly by day, these turtles eat mostly tadpoles, nymphs, seeds, leaves, fish, and aquatic plants. Their long snake-like necks are capable of swift lunging movements allowing them to snatch insects out of the air.

Snapping turtles have huge heads and powerful jaws. They are not gentle giants. Notorious for their nasty dispositions, they possess a great readiness to bite and can amputate a finger or toe in an instant.

Occasionally some well-meaning individual will attempt to pick up a snapper by its tail to get it out of the road before it gets run over, only to have it flail its head and snap its jaws every which way. This in not recommended. If it is a large turtle, picking it up by its tail damages its spinal column. All snappers should be held with the carapace toward your body, an arms length away, fingers as far from the long reaching head as possible. In general it is not wise to handle snapping turtles.

Unlike most turtles, snappers are unable to withdraw into their shells. Maybe that's why they look and act so ferocious. Many people consider soups and stews made from the flesh of snapping turtles great delicacies.

66

Bog Turtle

Bog turtles are rare in the Finger Lakes area. They are sometimes found in bogs, marshes, swamps, and slow moving streams with muddy bottoms where they feed on crayfish, frogs, worms, slugs, etc. They have become increasingly endangered as wetlands are drained for development.

Measuring only three to three and one-half inches they are one of the smallest species. The hatchlings are a mere one inch.

This little reptile is recognized by its yellow head patch.

The Mink

A mink is a sleek animal, larger and heavier than a weasel but with shorter legs. It has small ears, a white patch on its chin and partly webbed feet. The males, thirteen-to-seventeen-inches long, seven-to-nine-inches tall, and weighing one and one-half-to-three pounds, are about twenty-five percent larger than the females. Their tails are only slightly bushy. Minks, which have stiff hair webbing between their toes, are good swimmers and divers.

They build their nests in recesses beneath stones or tree roots or above ground in thickets of reeds, always near water. They sometimes inhabit old burrows or dens of other animals.

Having mated sometime from March to April, the female produces a litter of two to six young in April or May. It takes the kits about thirty days for their eyes to open. They are suckled for four to five weeks, are sexually mature at about nine months, and usually breed the first year.

A mink is a skillful, efficient hunter, surviving on rodents (voles, musk-rats), rabbits, moles, frogs, fishes, crustaceans, insects, birds, eggs, and plant material. They can do a lot of damage in a poultry house or a fish-breeding pond because, like their relative the weasel, they kill more than they can eat and cache the surplus.

If disturbed while feeding, a mink hisses and growls threateningly. Mink are quite common around the Finger Lakes but because they are very shy as well as mostly nocturnal they are not seen very often. You will know if they are around if you see the remains of their prey or, in winter, slides in the snow on the banks of streams, ponds, or lakes.

There is some variation in color among mink. Most have thick, lustrous, dark brown pelts. When real fur coats were in fashion, mink were one of the most luxurious and expensive. The animals are elusive and difficult to trap, so to meet the demand for their fur mink farms were established. By selective breeding "blond," "platinum," and "sapphire" pelts became popular.

A word of caution to those of you who like to fish: If you are lucky, or skillful enough to catch fish, it is not smart to toss your catch onto the bank and leave it unattended while you go on fishing. A stealthy mink can make away with your fish in a flash without you being aware of its presence.

An Efficient Killer — the Weasel

A weasel is a small animal with the reputation of being a sneaky, vicious, bloodthirsty predator that kills just for the sake of killing and that slaughters more prey at one time than it can possibly eat.

With small rounded ears, snub nose and inquisitive little black eyes, the weasel looks like an innocent and gentle creature, especially when it stands up on its hind legs and looks around. However, it is a highly efficient killer

One can't deny that a weasel is a rapacious carnivore. It's in almost non-stop motion and it takes a lot of fuel to meet its energy needs. It regularly eats over twenty-five percent of its body weight each day, hunting both night and day. Mice and other small mammals account for most of its diet. An adult rabbit is the largest prey it will normally attack. Overtaking its prey—it moves very fast—it straddles it, bites into the skull with its razor-sharp canine teeth and hangs on until the victim ceases to struggle. It drinks the victim's blood and eats its flesh.

When almost every farm had a hen house, more than one farmer went out in the morning to find many, if not all, of his chickens slaughtered. Occasionally the guilty little culprit, well sated, would be sleeping beside its kill, no doubt expecting to wake up to another good feed.

If the weasel stumbles onto a group of small mammals, such as a nest of young rabbits, it will quickly dispatch as many as it can catch, then eat and drink its fill. However, it does not waste the excess food. It catches it to be eaten at a time when the hunt is less productive.

There are two kinds of weasels around the Finger Lakes, the short-tailed which is about ten inches long, and the long-tailed which measures about fourteen. The long-tailed is the most widely distributed. Unless you see these two together it is hard to tell the difference. Both have slender, low-slung bodies, short legs, and plush fur. In summer they are brown with white underparts and feet. Their winter coat is pure white. The tip of the tail is black year-round. For centuries the white winter pelt of the weasel has been extremely valuable in the fur trade where it is known as ermine (technically, it is the short tail weasel that is true ermine).

Weasels live close to water, denning in abandoned burrows of other small animals or under wood or rock piles. The males, which are noticeably larger than the females, mate at one year while the females start at three or four months. They mate in early to mid-summer. A litter of about four to eight kits is born in late April or early May of the following year in a nest of grass, leaves, and fur. They suckle for six weeks, the latter part of which the mother gives them small bits of soft meat. Like a mother cat, she then brings them live prey. Soon they are following after her, learning to stalk and kill. Weasels are solitary. The few months the kits are with the mother are their only social life.

The mother keeps in contact with her young by trilling. Weasels also shriek, usually when agitated or cornered or when seizing prey; sometimes when mating.

Territorial, an adult male patrols his area and marks it with secretions from a set of glands near the anus. The foul-smelling musk warns off other males.

Weasels survive because they are fierce and adaptable. However, even they fall prey to hawks and owls. I know of one that was stomped to death when he invaded the cage of my neighbor's big tame Australian gray rabbit. They are also susceptible to a variety of diseases including distemper and rabies.

Skunk Babies Arrive

There are four kinds of skunks in North America but the striped is the only one found around the Finger Lakes. You may hear it called a "polecat" but that is a misnomer; a polecat is a European ferret.

Skunks are long-furred animals about the size of a house cat. They are black with a narrow white stripe up the middle of the forehead and a broad white area at the nape of the neck which usually splits into a V over the shoulders, and continuing back to the tail which may or may not have a white tip. There is much variation in the length and width of stripes between individuals. Some skunks have little white — others more white than black. In the fur trade the mostly black ones have always been the most valuable, frequently marketed as "black martin" or "Hudson Bay Sable."

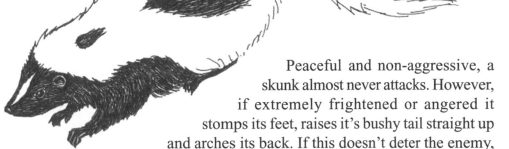

Peaceful and non-aggressive, a skunk almost never attacks. However, if extremely frightened or angered it stomps its feet, raises it's bushy tail straight up and arches its back. If this doesn't deter the enemy, the skunk curls into a U and lets fly with an oily, amber-colored, extremely foul smelling liquid from its two scent glands, one on either side of the anus. The skunk aims for the enemy's face, and its effective range is about twelve feet. For an animal whose usual gait is slow and waddling, the skunk can launch an amazingly fast attack.

Skunks are nocturnal and omnivorous, dining on mice, grubs, eggs, berries, insects, and carrion. They feast on wasps and bees without appearing to feel their stings. Occasionally they raid poultry houses.

Ground burrows beneath old buildings, boulders, rock piles, or wood piles serve as family dens to skunks. The males are solitary, but several females often den together during the winter. Not true hibernators, they sleep a lot but are often out on warm nights in the middle of winter.

Skunks mate in February or March and five or six young are born in early May. They are the size of field mice and blind. At the age of eight weeks they are digging up grubs and batting down beetles, bees, and grasshoppers with their big paws. The babies always follow their mother in single file.

Homeowners are sometimes exasperated by skunks rooting up their lawns in search of grubs. However, they also destroy many small rodents and harmful insects.

In early days when hospitals were few and far between and antibiotics unheard of, rendered skunk oil, rubbed on one's chest, was thought to be the best way to prevent pneumonia.

Skunks have but one natural predator, the great horned owl. Flying on silent wings, the owl can attack and kill the skunk before it has a chance to muster its defenses.

A few years ago I was trying to evict a female raccoon who had had her babies in my chimney. I called a wildlife control person who set a trap in my backyard. It was box-like, designed so that a door came down if an animal entered it. The next morning I saw that the door was down. He came, prepared to haul away a raccoon. I was surprised when he stopped suddenly a few feet from the trap. He went and got a long pole from his pickup and carefully maneuvered the end of it until he managed to raise the door. He moved very slowly, and several times I heard him say softly, "It's all right little skunky."

Uneasily, I kept waiting for the skunk's odor to foul the air around my house. But it didn't happen. The wildlife man tied a rope to his pole and tied the rope to my bird feeder to hold the door open so the skunk could leave. But the skunk had other plans, he waddled back to the farthest corner of the trap, curled up and went to sleep. Fortunately, by the next morning he was gone. Unfortunately, the raccoon was still there!

The Ferns

Ferns grow in damp, shady places. The woods and the rocky glens of the Finger Lakes region are ideal habitats for many of them.

Most ferns look like what we think ferns should look like — feathery, with lacy fronds. The hart's tongue and the walking fern, however, look a lot like other green plants and often are not commonly recognized as ferns. I touch on but a few of the most common ferns you will encounter around the Finger Lakes. Using a good field guide, such as Peterson's or Wherry's, you will discover others.

Ferns thrive in clusters, spreading by spores, minute dust-like grains on the undersides of their fronds that are scattered by the wind.

With the exception of the Christmas fern which is green year-round, ferns, like the leaves of trees, turn red, yellow and brown in the fall. Eventually the fronds fall to the ground and decay.

In early spring new fronds appear. They look like little curled-up balls. As they grow they unroll and spread out into lace-like fronds. The young rolled-up ferns, called fiddleheads, sometimes are eaten as greens, and are considered a delicacy.

Maidenhair Spleenwort

With delicate, uniform, dark green fronds from two to eight inches long that form a rosette, maidenhair spleenwort is one of the most beautiful ferns of the Finger Lakes area. It can be found in moist, sheltered crevices or in cavernous places in rocks, often along the rocky lakeshores. It remains green all year.

Maidenhair Fern

The maidenhair fern has a slender, shiny dark brown, terminally forked stalk. Its delicate fronds and slender stalks were believed by the Romans to be the hair of Venus, goddess of love and beauty, perhaps because under water they take on a silvery sheen yet are perfectly dry when removed. The Romans made a potion from the powdered fern which they believed would produce beauty and love.

Maidenhair fern is common on wooded slopes in the humus-rich soils of our region.

73

Marginal Wood Fern

Easily recognized by the small brown dots along the margins of the lobes which contain the spores, the marginal wood fern grows from twelve to thirty inches tall in rocky woods and on shaded ledges.

Interupted Fern

When you run across a bunch of interrupted ferns you will know immediately what you have found, their name is so appropriate. Near the middle of the fronds are dark green to brown clusters of spore cases which wither away early in the season leaving the frond "interrupted."

Thirty to sixty inches tall, these plants grow on wooded slopes, along swamp margins, and in open thickets.

Christmas Fern

The Christmas fern looks much like a Boston fern only it has a narrow bulge near the stem on each lobe of the frond which, if you have a good imagination, looks like the toe of a Christmas stocking. It is evergreen, grows twelve to thirty inches tall, and likes humus-rich crevices.

Bracken Fern

Bracken is a tall coarse fern, masses of which grow profusely in neglected meadows and open woodland around the Finger Lakes.

Unlike most other ferns, bracken thrives in both sun and shade, so it isn't likely you will find it in the moist, shady glens of the lakes. The leaves are broad and thicker than the delicate fronds of most other ferns. Because it is sturdy and durable, bracken is sometimes used as bedding for animals.

Ostrich Fern

The ostrich fern is the tallest fern in the area, growing from twenty inches to six and one-half feet. It likes wet soil and is often found in swamps. The fronds are narrow at the base, widening at the top, giving it an ostrich-like appearance. The ostrich fern is commonly gathered for food in the spring.

New York (Tapering Fern)

The twelve-to-sixty-inch New York fern has fronds that taper at both the bottom and the top. The fronds are a yellowish green, thin and deciduous. Common throughout the Finger Lakes area, they grow in moist woods, swamps, and thickets.

75

A Brief Respite

The Finger Lakes lie between two major flyways, the coastal down the Atlantic coast and the Mississippi River down the center of the country. With lots of water and a good food supply, many migrating birds stop to feed and rest during their long journeys. At least 235 different species have been recorded at the Montezuma National Wildlife Refuge at the north end of Cayuga Lake since it was established in 1937.

Birds around the Finger Lakes vary in size from the tiny ruby-throated hummingbird to the big wild turkey. The first birds to arrive in the spring are red-winged blackbirds, robins, woodcock, and killdeer. Early May brings migrating warblers, hyperkinetic little flashes of color that constantly flit from branch to branch.

Birds of the same species vary in color depending on their sex and the time of year. During the breeding season they take on vivid colorations. As a rule, the males are the brightest. However, ground nesters of both sexes have mottled plumage for camouflage.

Naturalists think birds sing to lay claim to a territory. Other bird behavior is less understood. Why do some birds eat seeds while others are carnivores? Why are some promiscuous while others mate for life? Why does the brown-headed cowbird lay her eggs in other birds' nests and abandon them whereas most birds incubate their

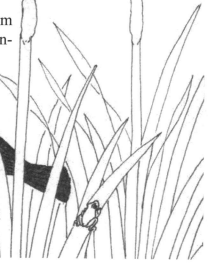

eggs and nurture the young to fledging or beyond?

Birds have well-developed brains and ears on the sides of their heads much like ours only covered with feathers. They are able to detect worms crawling underground by sounds too low pitched for us to hear. They can also feel the vibrations in their feet.

You've probably heard someone with a dainty appetite described as "eating like a bird." Well, a bird eats its own weight in food every day. A young robin eats up to fourteen feet of earthworms a day.

An Exquisite Beauty

With black wings edged with two rows of yellow spots and hind wings with a submarginal blue band, many think the black swallowtail is the most exquisite butterfly in the Finger Lakes Region. The female has more blue, and is the more striking.

A little bit smaller than the tiger swallowtail, the black swallowtail is common and widespread. These will be the two swallowtails you are sure to see. They both frequent fields, gardens, open spaces, and roadsides. They often gather in groups and spend the night together. The males cluster at puddles and are affectionately dubbed "mud puddle clubs" by butterfly enthusiasts.

The larvae are green with black bands with small yellow spots. They can be pests in the garden feeding on parsley, celery, carrots, dill, and caraway. They also eat wild carrot. They spend the winter as pupae in a brown chrysalis. There are two broods each year. The first brood is smaller with larger yellow spots than the later one. In mid-May the adults emerge to impress the lucky observer.

77

Fireflies

Fireflies, or lightning bugs as they are sometimes called, are not really flies at all, but members of the beetle family known as lampridae. Those indigenous to the Finger Lakes measure about one-half- inch in length.

Twinkling in the dusk like tiny erratic stars, fireflies lend enchantment to June evenings around the Finger Lakes. A child may catch a few, put them in a glass jar and take them into their dark bedroom and marvel at the amount of light the little creatures produce. However, the females are larger than the males and tend to be predacious. Often there are fewer fireflies to release in the morning than went into the jar the night before.

You can find fireflies nearly everywhere. There are at least fifty species of them in the United States. In the Finger Lakes region, they tend to congregate in the greatest numbers where the humidity is high: over swales, around ponds, along the banks of rivers, streams, and lakes; above damp meadows and over marshes.

If you were to examine one of these beguiling little lamplighters in daylight, you would find it has a tail section that resembles a miniature pale green Chinese lantern. This lantern contains two substances, luciferin and luciferase, both of which are manufactured by the creature's own cells. Light is produced when the luciferin, in the presence of sun-light and water, unites with oxygen. The luciferase is the catalyst that starts the process and keeps it going. When the luciferin is burned, it is not used up, but changed back to its original state, and the firefly is ready to produce another flash. Thus, it has a constant supply of light.

The firefly's flash lasts less than one-half-second; several seconds elapse between flashes. There are over 2,000 species of fireflies in the world. Each has its own flash "code." Fireflies flash to attract mates. The males flit low over the ground—seldom above 25 feet—flashing signals to the females which are perched on low growing vegetation beneath them. When a male spots an answering flash from the ground, he drops down and after a series of exchanged flashes, if the signals match, mating occurs.

As a rule, a firefly will respond only to the flash code of another firefly of the same species. Rarely, a female of one species will lure a male of a different species by imitating that species' flash code; them kill him.

Some naturalists believe that nonsynchronous fireflies use their flashes not only to attract mates, but as a warning to bats, birds and other nocturnal predators which learn after one experience that bugs that light up may be pretty but they taste awful.

The fireflies' display is a seasonal one. Around the Finger Lakes region it begins in early June and lasts through July. For them to begin flashing, they require temperatures ranging from sixty-eight to eighty degrees. They live on a twenty-four-hour cycle. Creatures of the dusk, they do not perform well in bright moonlight or in absolute darkness

It is safe to handle a firefly. It will not bite, sting, or burn you. Unlike that made by man, the firefly's light is cold. It has the greenish tinge of phosphorescence, but is actually a bioluminescence with a luminous efficiency of ninety percent, the most efficient known. Compare it to an incandescent lamp, which has a luminous efficiency of ten percent.

As an adult, a firefly lives about one month. After mating, the female lays her eggs in the ground. The following spring the eggs hatch, the larvae make their way to the surface where they bite, poison, and feed on snails, slugs, and earthworms. In the fall they build tiny mud homes where they spend the winter.

During their second spring, the larvae outgrow their skins, shed them and become pupae. Some ten days later, these pupae shed their skins to become adult fireflies.

The first night as a firefly, the beetle hardens and strengthens. The second night, it tests its flashing apparatus. By the third night it is ready to find a mate.

Centuries ago, the firefly's light was studied by the Greek philosopher, Aristotle, and by Pliny, the Roman author and student of natural history.

More recently, fireflies have been the subject of intensive laboratory investigation by the Department of Neurobiology at Cornell University, at John Hopkins University, at the University of Florida, and at the Sigma Chemical Company of St. Louis. So far none of these scientists have been able to duplicate the firefly's light in their laboratories.

Nature lovers are still captivated by the mystique of these little lamp-lighters.

Winter Babies

The black bear is the smallest and most plentiful of all bears in the United States. Once killed for their gall bladders, which Eastern cultures prized for medicinal purposes, and for their paws for making bear paw soup, at one time their numbers fell drastically. Then game laws were enacted and enforced and the bears came back.

Black bears display much variation in character and habits. Most are peaceful and easy—going. However, they are wild and unpredictable even though they may look cute and cuddly like the teddy bear which, incidentally, turned one hundred in the year 2002. Zookeepers agree that black bears are among the most shrewd and intelligent animals with which they deal.

In the last few years sightings of black bears have become common around the Finger Lakes, around Mecklenburg, Alpine, Cayutaville, and Newfield particularly. Area residents are seeing them along roads, in their backyards, occasionally on their back porches, and robbing their bird feeders.

Black bears are eclectic in their eating habits. Though classified as carnivores (flesh eaters), their teeth are suitable for either tearing flesh or grinding vegetable matter. Their diets consist of grass, grain, roots, nuts, fruit, grubs, insects, snails, crabs, frogs, snakes, eggs, fish, and carrion. Their fondness for ants and honey is legendary. An adult black bear's fur is so thick it is impenetrable to bee stings, but the muzzles of both young and very old are vulnerable.

A black bear may live for fifteen to twenty-five years. It reaches sexual maturity when it is two to three years old. June to July is the breeding season. The bears, especially the males, wander about, leaving scratch marks on trees to let other bears know that they have been there. A small bear alone or with another bear of comparable size is probably a two-year-old whose mother has abandoned him as the mating season arrived. One-year-old cubs travel with their mother during the summer and autumn, and sleep with her during the next winter. Sows breed only every other year.

Both sexes hibernate, each in its own den. The female is more selective about her site. Her cubs will need to be protected from rain, snow, and driving wind; the entrance to the den is well hidden. Winter quarters may be a hollow tree, a cave, or a den which the animal scoops out for itself.

Unlike most wild creatures, black bear embryos do not begin growing immediately after mating. Until late fall they lie dormant within the female. As she begins her winter's sleep they begin to grow.

The female gives birth in mid-January, during a state of semi-hibernation, to a litter of from one to three cubs. They are about the size of squirrels. The babies grow slowly. By the end of their second week they have developed a thick coat of fur. However, their eyes are not open until they are a month old. When they are about three months old they are able to leave the den with their mother.

The black bear is very hungry when it awakes from its long sleep and in the fall when it must put on enough fat to sustain it through the winter.

81

An adult black bear stands about three feet at the shoulder, and is approximately five to six feet long. The male weighs from 150 to 300 pounds; the female is usually a little smaller. The male lives longer, possibly because he has only himself to care for and does not take part in raising cubs. The female feeds and cares for the young and teaches them the skills they will need to survive in the wild. The cubs remain with their mother for about two years .

Black bears are very adaptable. With sharp, curled claws, they are skillful tree climbers. No human can climb as fast. And though their gait makes them appear clumsy, one can gallop fast enough to overtake the fastest human runner—about 35 mph. It's not wise to try boxing with one either. It can stand on its hind legs and deliver a killing blow with its front paws.

The Mosquitoes Return

Over one hundred species of mosquitoes live in the United States. The most common around the Finger Lakes is the ordinary house mosquito.

The house mosquito breeds in stagnant water. In May or June the female lays her eggs in boat-shaped masses of from one hundred to four hundred eggs on or immediately under the water. Each tiny egg is boat-shaped and has air chambers like pontoons on its sides. The eggs hatch in one to three days. The larval period, during which the insect eats, grows, and molts, usually lasts seven to ten days, and up to three weeks if the weather is unseasonably cold.

During the two to three day pupal stage, the pupa rests right side up near the surface of the water using a snorkel-like tube to get air. During this period it does not eat.

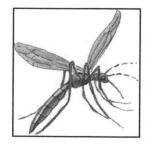

The adult males emerge first. They hover waiting for the females to emerge for mating. The male mosquito keeps a low profile, feeds on plant juices, and is seldom seen. The female also feeds on plant nectar, but she requires a blood meal, animal or human, to produce viable eggs. She's the one you hear buzzing around your ear. Her buzz has a frequency peculiar to her particular species so she may be looking for a mate as well as a meal. The males have plume-like antennae which serve as ears to locate humming females. After mating the males live about a week.

Mosquitoes have built-in heat detection systems in their front legs, and are attracted to body warmth circulating on air currents. They are also attracted by the carbon dioxide exhaled by breathing. Insect repellent works by clogging the pores of the insect's chemoreceptors, blocking their sensory perceptions. House mosquitoes are night biters.

In studies, researchers found that mosquitoes will bother you more if you wear dark clothing. During their experiments, only one-tenth as many of them lit on white material.

The female mosquito bites by pushing her feeding tube through the victim's skin and into a capillary. She then injects an anti-coagulant to keep the blood from clotting. With the house mosquito, the result is just an annoying itch. With certain other species, however, the pathogens in their saliva can cause serious illness.

The Anopheles mosquito is a carrier of malaria. During the building of the Erie Canal (1817-1825) through the Montezuma Swamp at the north end of Cayuga Lake, the disease killed hundreds of workers. In recent years there have been no known cases in the area.

A few specimens of another harmful strain of mosquitoes, the Aedes, are still found occasionally in Cicero Swamp near Syracuse. This carries the equine encephalitis pathogen which has been known to kill horses, and rarely, humans. If a female mosquito bites an infected animal, her bite remains infectious throughout her life, which is about a month. If the numbers warrant it, the swamp is sprayed, but that practice is not without controversy.

Mosquitoes are eaten by bats, dragonflies, frogs, snakes, birds, and fish.

A few years ago, when an unusually large numbers of dead birds, mostly crows, were found around the area, local Health Departments investigated and discovered the birds had been killed by the West Nile virus, a disease caused by the bite of an infected mosquito. A few humans were found to have the disease and officials advised people to stay indoors in the early evening when mosquitoes feed most, to cover up their bodies as much as possible, to repair holes in their screens, and to apply insect repellent containing Deet.

JUNE

June is the beginning of summer; the favorite month of those who live around the Finger Lakes. Almost every wild flowering plant is in bloom in June. Nature's wild babies venture out to explore their new world. Birdsong fills the long summer days. Wild strawberries ripen.

Fawns Arrive

By the first of June most of the pregnant white-tailed does around the Finger Lakes have dropped their fawns. They don't build dens or nests but give birth in areas of dense brush or tall, thick weeds. Single births are the most common, however, twins are not unusual and occasionally there are triplets. At birth a fawn weighs about fifteen to twenty pounds. In the case of triplets, each baby will be somewhat smaller. The doe hides her baby in dense vegetation while she feeds nearby. Now and then she gives a soft lowing sound. The fawn, light brown with lighter-colored tan spots, is well-camouflaged in the sun and shade-mottled environment.

It takes the newborn fawn about twelve hours to get on its feet. It gives off no scent during its first week or so of life, nature's way of protecting it from predators such as the coyote and the black bear which rely on their keen sense of smell to locate prey. For about a week, until it is strong enough to travel with its mother, the fawn lies motionless on the ground, almost as if its mother had told it to not move. About every four hours the doe returns to nurse her baby. She leaves as soon as the little one gets its fill of milk so any predator will not get her scent. If another wild animal does approach, the doe will try to distract it away from the fawn. Gradually, the fawns spots disappear; and within a year they are completely gone.

If you stumble upon a lone fawn, don't assume its mother has died or abandoned it. That's almost certainly not the case. Don't try to pet or handle a fawn. Some people believe that a doe will reject her baby if it gets the scent of a human on it.

The Intelligent Raccoon

Raccoons are good swimmers and like to be near water. Perhaps that's why we have so many of them around the Finger Lakes. Because they have been observed dunking their food in water before eating it, they have the reputation of being extremely clean. However, they also have been seen eating earthworms loaded with dirt.

Almost anything pleases the raccoon palate: nuts, earthworms, baby birds, baby rabbits, snails, crayfish, grapes, berries, eggs, frogs, lizards, crickets, tadpoles, mussels, grasshoppers, caterpillars, minnows, and garbage. They are one of the few animals that will even eat a toad.

Quite likely it is their omnivorous traits and adaptability to development which has helped raccoons thrive at a time when some other animals are on the decline. Then too, in the wild, they have few natural enemies and those—the bobcat, lynx, and cougar—are extremely rare in our area. Man is their chief predator. Though not as much as in years past when they were hunted for their pelts. A large number are killed on the highways. Nevertheless, worldwide, the raccoon population has remained fairly steady for centuries.

An adult raccoon weighs from ten to thirty pounds. Their paws look surprisingly like human hands, with a thumb and four digits. Your first encounter with a raccoon may occur some night when you are awakened by the clatter of garbage cans. These night-time marauders will eat just about anything you toss out. Besides being able to pry the lids off garbage cans, raccoons will tear off shingles, roofing, and screens to get into your attic. The females often choose attics and chimneys in which to rear their young. They are not easy to evict. They are clever at eluding you and, if cornered, extremely fierce fighters. However, raccoons love peanut butter, and more than one beleaguered householder has spread it on crackers to lure an offending raccoon into a trap to be carted off to a faraway woods.

In the wild, raccoons den in hollow trees, piles of rocks, and sometimes ground dens, usually near water.
About the first of May, the female raccoon gives birth to three or four young. Relatives of the lesser panda, the babies are adorable little creatures with a bandit-like mask and ringed tails like their parents. The young leave their mother when they are about a year old and start their own families when they are two to three. They can live to be twelve years old, but their average lifespan in the wild averages about five years.

In the fall raccoons feed heavily, putting on twenty-five percent of their total weight including a one-inch-thick layer of fat on its rump. Their predilection for late-summer sweet corn is legendary. They seem to know to the minute when the ears have reached their optimum succulence. Many a gardener has gone to bed at night only to get up in the morning and find his ready-to-eat corn field devastated. About the only thing that will keep the critters out is a properly installed electric fence. I know a few

87

gardeners who plant pumpkins in their corn and train the vines around the perimeter of the patch. They say the raccoons do not like to go through the prickly vines because their fur catches on them.

Raccoons spend the winter sleeping in hollow trees. The entrance of the nest averages twenty-six feet above the ground though the nest itself may be as much as eleven feet down inside the trunk. Not true hibernators, when the temperature gets up to about twenty-eight degrees, they come out in search of food.

Deadly fights are avoided by using raccoon etiquette. For instance, a single raccoon approaching a strange group appears timid and nervous. Sometimes it will back toward the others to avoid confrontation.

Periodically an epidemic of rabies thins the raccoon population. It is a very serious problem because other animals they come in contact with also become infected. If you encounter a raccoon, especially in the daytime, that is acting strange—unusually tame, overly aggressive, lethargic—keep your distance even if the animal looks healthy. In its early stages rabies shows no symptoms.

Raccoons are among the most intelligent mammals. They learn quickly and have good memories, which improve with age. In one experiment research teams presented them with a latch-type puzzle. The first try took them seventeen minutes to solve it, the second try, four. On the fifth and succeeding tries they were able to work the puzzle in two seconds. Furthermore, a year later, when presented with the same puzzle, they repeated the two-second solution.

Dragonflies

Dragonflies are active on the warm, sunny days of June around the Finger Lakes. Seeing one at rest on a water lily is a real treat. There are several species of dragonflies throughout the area. The largest and most common is the green darner which has a shimmering green thorax, a brown abdomen trimmed with blue, four long, clear, glassy wings, and two huge compound eyes that take up most of its head. Ten spot dragonflies, distinguished by the black spots on their clear wings, are common also.

Ponds and slow-moving streams are favorite haunts for these insects. They are territorial. An adult male will chase and attack another male and drive him away. One male displays his dominance over another by raising his abdomen. A dragonfly's abdomen is slender, and about two inches long. At one time people believed it was made for stinging. It's not. Only other insects need fear the dragonfly.

When resting, the dragonfly holds its wings out horizontally at right angles to its body. Dragonflies are most active on warm, sunny days. Mealtimes are early mornings and late afternoons. A savage hunter, the green darner can travel up to 45 mph. With great dexterity, a dragonfly pursues its prey, then snatches it out of the air with its powerful jaws.

Small insects like mosquitoes, its main prey, are eaten on the wing. Larger ones such as butterflies and bees are taken to a nearby perch to be devoured. If a dragonfly is interrupted during its meal it seldom leaves its food behind. Usually it simply carries it to another spot and resumes eating. A dragonfly has an enormous appetite, rivaled only by that of the praying mantis. One was observed eating forty flies in less than two hours.

Naturalists believe the dragonfly's antennae are organs of taste, touch, smell, and hearing and are unusually well developed. If the insect loses its antennae it is virtually helpless.

Unlike most other insects which go through four stages of development—egg, larva or nymph, pupa, and adult—the dragonfly goes through only three: egg, nymph, and adult.

Dragonflies mate in late summer. The female lays thousands of eggs just beneath the surface of the water, sometimes while still clutched by the male. The eggs soon hatch into nymphs — short, flattened, hard-shelled creatures without wings. They survive the winter in the soft bottom mud of the water in which the eggs were laid, breathing through gills like fish.

They remain in the nymph stage one to two years feeding on a variety of smaller insects and insect larvae, tadpoles, and even each other. In May, those ready to become adults climb out of the water and very slowly creep up the stem of an aquatic plant or onto a stone where they make a final molt. They must wait an hour or two for their bodies to harden and their wings to dry before they can fly. During this period they are particularly vulnerable to swallows, kingbirds, some small hawks, frogs, snakes, and fish.

You can enjoy dragonflies only from spring to fall. They are killed by the first frost.

Damselflies

Damselflies are smaller and more delicate in structure than their larger relatives the dragonfly. They have thin, brightly colored black, blue, green, and red bodies and two pairs of gossamer wings of nearly equal size. The black-winged has a metallic green body about one-and three-quarter-inches long. Of the many varieties, most damselflies around the Finger Lakes have dark bodies and clear blue wings.

Not as swift and powerful a flier as the dragonfly, the damselfly darts and flutters low over a thick growth of weeds and water plants. You are likely to see them in a habitat of spatterdock and pickerelweed. They like still water.

You can tell a damselfly from its larger relative by the way it holds its wings folded together over its back when resting. The male likes to rest on a sprig of leaves in the sun, slowly opening his wings, and then quickly snapping them shut.

The female sometimes cleans her eyes and antennae with her forelegs, like a cat washing its face.

The damselfly feeds mostly on mosquitoes, midges, gnats, and other small insects. Though a weak flyer, it is a fierce predator.

90

Like the dragonfly, damselflies go through but three stages of development. They mate in late summer. The female lays her eggs on flotsam, leaves, or plant stems just beneath the surface of the water. Sometimes it's a joint project. The male grasps the thorax of the female and they fly through the air hooked together until they submerge.

The damselfly nymph differs from that of the dragonfly. Instead of gills, it has an appendage like a snorkel with which to extract oxygen. The nymph stage of the damselfly approximates that of the dragonfly, and the final molt occurs in the same manner.

Mulberry

The red, or American, mulberry is native to the eastern United States. It has been around for a long time. Carbon dating was done on a sharpened mulberry stake found wedged between the upper and lower shell of a now extinct, 12,000-year-old tortoise shell.

Mulberry is quite widespread around the Finger Lakes. Some of the trees produce one-inch-long white fruits; others purple. Mulberries bloom in late spring. In our area, the fruit ripens in the June sunshine. The catkin-like flowers are small, clustered, and greenish. Eaten mostly by birds and wild animals, these days they are mostly ignored by humans. However, for about two decades, roughly from 1830 to 1850, the mulberry just might have received the most interest of any tree growing in our entire area.

As gold fever hit California, the silk craze engulfed the Finger Lakes. The mania transcended all social classes, and many formerly sensible men planted hundreds of mulberry trees intending to get rich on the labors of their wives and children who would tend the silkworms while they (the men) went about their usual business.

The village of Fairport's first industry was a mulberry grove for raising silkworms, with an adjacent silk factory. And in the spring of 1837, near Auburn, a

91

man by the name of David West planted two thousand young mulberry trees, procured a quantity of the eggs of the silkworm, and built cocooneries. Other entrepreneurs in the same area also went into the silk business.

At that time the state was looking for some industry to occupy the convicts at Auburn prison. In May 1841, the New York State Legislature authorized the manufacture of silk by the inmates. However, the male convicts lacked the delicate touch the operation required.

In a few years it became evident throughout the area, and elsewhere, that it was impossible for Americans to master the fine technique of silk culture or to compete with the cheap labor of the Orient and Europe.

In the beginning many would-be silk producers believed, mistakenly, that silkworms would eat the leaves of any mulberry, including the native red, a medium-sized tree with dark brown fissured and scaly bark and purple fruit. They wouldn't.

There is a red mulberry that produces fruit on the east side of the Potomac Road in the Finger Lakes National Forest about a mile south of the Searsburg Road in Schuyler County.

On the south side of the Lodi Station Road about a mile west of the Village of Lodi in Seneca County there is a medium-sized white mulberry tree.

The wood of the native mulberry is very heavy and was used locally for fence posts, cooperage, furniture, and agricultural implements.

Mulberry wood is not good to burn in your fireplace. Heat causes it to send out sparks like a Fourth of July rocket.

The Majestic Eagle

The bald eagle is uniquely American; unknown in the Old World. Considered a symbol of freedom, in 1782, the Continental Congress chose the bird as our national emblem. Thomas Jefferson described it as a "free spirit. high-soaring and courageous." In Jefferson's time there were about a half million of them were on the wing in the skies of North America.

During the first half of the twentieth century, ranchers and farmers who thought the eagles were a menace to their livestock killed huge numbers of them. However, inasmuch as the most an eagle can carry is about six pounds, they were a very small threat to domestic farm animals.

Finally, realizing the questionable survival of the bald eagle, in 1940, Congress enacted the Bald Eagle Protection Act, which made it illegal to kill, harass, possess, or sell the bird. Still their numbers decreased. In 1967, with only 417 known breeding pairs left in the continental United States, the bird was placed on the endangered species list, victims of the insecticide DDT which accumulated in their main food source: fish.

With the banning of DDT, the eagles made an impressive comeback. Now there are about 6,000 known nesting pairs in the continental United States. In the year 2,000, the bald eagle was removed from the endangered species list.

Bald eagles are rare around the Finger Lakes. However, thanks to a vigorous effort by Cornell University, a few of them are soaring again in the sky over the Montezuma National Wildlife Refuge and the northern end of Cayuga Lake. In fact, recently a resident along the lake reported to the Laboratory of Ornithology at Cornell that he had seen an immature eagle attack a young Canada goose.

An adult bald eagle weighs about ten pounds. Black-feathered, with a wingspan of six to seven feet tip to tip, and with both a white head and tail, it is a distinctive creature. It is sometimes confused with the more common osprey, another large bird with a white head. The osprey, however, doesn't have a white tail.

Bald eagles mate for life and return to the same nesting site year after year. Each year they add to the nest. What started out as a three-foot structure can reach up to eight feet.

Bald eagles usually build their nests in the tops of trees or up on a cliff. Their first nest in the Montezuma wildlife refuge was human-built. Visible from a tower beside one of the roads in the refuge, birders watched ecstatically as the first pair of eagles took up residency.

Bald eagles usually raise two to three chicks per year. The female incubates the eggs; the male feeds and protects her. Both parents provide food for their ravenous young. The eaglets are balls of fluffy white down. Gradually they get their dark feathers and it takes from three to five years for their heads to turn white.

About two years ago a savage windstorm tore through the area and the nest was blown away. The eagles survived, but moved deeper into the marshes and built their own nest. According to the Laboratory of Ornithology at Cornell, there are currently four active nests in Montezuma. They cannot be seen from the road.

In the wild, eagles live about ten to fifteen years; in captivity, twenty-five to thirty.

A Spider's Life

Although often called so, spiders are not insects. They belong to a different group called arachnids. All insects have six legs, where spiders have eight. An insect has a segmented body divided into three parts. A spider's body has two parts: a fused head and thorax, and an abdomen. Insects have antennae; spiders have two claw-like appendages at the front of their heads which they use for seizing prey.

Spiders are nature's spinners and weavers; their webs are marvels of creation. In Greek mythology, the spider started out as a girl named Arachne. Athena, the Greek goddess of wisdom, was greatly skilled as a weaver. One day Arachne bragged that she could weave as well as the goddess. So Athena changed the girl into a spider which, according to legend, still lives to weave the wonderful webs we see on bushes and grasses today.

Depending on the species, spiders may have from two to eight eyes, one type suited for night vision; others adapted to daylight.

A spider's leg is made up of seven segments and ends in two or three small, sharp claws. It has four pairs of legs attached to the thorax.

Near the rear on the underside of the spider's abdomen are (usually) three pairs of tubelike organs, called spinnerets, through which silk is expelled from the body. The fine silk thread, about four thousandths of an inch in diameter, is liquid when it leaves the spider's body, but coagulates when it comes into contact with the air.

Only the female builds webs. She produces two kinds of silk, a

dry, inelastic thread for making the framework, center, and spokes and a sticky, elastic one that clings to anything it touches.

The spirals of the web on which prey are to be entangled are made of the elastic silk thread, which she studs with little sticky beads. The spider herself scurries about on the framework, spokes and center pulling the threads to test their strength. She avoids the sticky spirals.

Sometimes a heavy rain or strong wind destroys the web and the spider has to rebuild it or go hungry.

You've probably seen a spider dangling in mid-air on the end of a tiny thread, which grows in length as she drops. She can also jump from one support to another as she attaches strands of her web. A spider can bridge several feet, even a small stream, by climbing to a high branch, waiting until the wind is in the right direction, then releasing a long thread which is carried to shrubs on the other side and becomes entangled there. She draws the strand tight and fastens it, then proceeds with the other lines.

All spiders do not weave beautiful doily-like webs. Some are funnel shaped, while others look like tissue paper. Some spiders do not make webs at all.

Once her web is finished, the spider usually retires to a hiding place, maybe a crack or under a leaf. When a victim becomes entangled in the web, it struggles, alerting the spider which runs out to secure it. Usually she swaths it in silk as she injects poison into it from her fangs. A spider cannot eat solid food. The poison not only paralyzes the prey, it acts as a digestive juice that liquefies the contents of its body. Later the spider injects its fangs into the victim's body and uses them to suck out the liquid.

The common orange or yellow garden spider you see all around the Finger Lakes waits for prey in the center of her web. Some other spiders hide in little woven nests near their snares. When a victim flies or jumps into the web, the lines jerk, the spider flashes out, quickly swaths it in silken thread, bites and poisons it and sucks it dry, leaving only the shell.

Courtship for a male spider can be chancy. All spiders live by eating mostly insects. The female is much larger than the male and if he gets too close to the female when she is hungry, he can end up as a meal, not a mate. If he loses only a leg, he will merely grow a new one. However, when you consider that the female builds her own house, catches her own food and looks after the young, is it any wonder she looks upon the male as somewhat dispensable?

In autumn the female spider lays her eggs in dingy yellowish cocoons containing six hundred to eight hundred eggs. She fastens the cocoon under leaves, a window sill, a plank or some other secluded corner. The spiderlings hatch the following June and immediately spin a sort of nest of fine silk strands in which they cluster for a few days before scattering. Each then spins a two-inch web.

Around the Finger Lakes, by November, most adult spiders have died. A few may survive in sheltered places such as the basement of a house. Spiders destroy millions of harmful insects: houseflies, mosquitoes, grasshoppers. They, in turn, are preyed upon by parasitic wasps and ants.

Brown Recluse Spider

The brown recluse spider is an unwelcome newcomer to the Finger Lakes area. Poisonous, its bite causes deep tissue and muscle damage. If left untreated, the wound becomes gangrenous, and can result in amputation of a limb. Rarely is it fatal.

Initially the bite is usually painless. In a day or two, however, it will have a black center around which a red, white, and blue bull's-eye pattern develops. The victim can suffer flu-like symptoms such as general weakness, aching, headache, nausea, and painful swelling. The wound can take from six months to a year to heal, and can leave quite a crater. If the poison eats into an artery it can cause unstoppable bleeding requiring immediate medical treatment.

In the first few cases of brown recluse bites around the Finger Lakes, diagnosis and treatment were delayed because, when puzzled doctors consulted the poison control centers around the country, they were told those arachnids lived only where temperatures ranged between 40° and 110° Fahrenheit. However, in 1993, in the Finger Lakes area, several people were treated for confirmed brown recluse bites. It is believed the spiders first arrived in the area as hitchhikers in travelers' luggage.

A brown recluse's body measures about one-quarter of an inch. Including its legs, which are noticeably spindly, the spider is about the size of a nickel. On the upper part it has a light tan-colored, violin-shaped marking.

As its name suggests, the creature is reclusive, hiding in dark basements, sheds, and closets. Outdoors, the nature lover could encounter it under a rock or log, in a woodpile, or in a cabin or outhouse. You should look carefully under the seat of any outdoor toilet before sitting down.

Daddy Longlegs (Harvester, Harvestman)

Daddy longlegs — or granddaddy longlegs as it is sometimes called —is not a spider, but a close relative of the order *Opiliones*. Daddy longlegs have one body section and a segmented abdomen, whereas a spider has two body sections and a non-segmented body; daddy longlegs have two eyes, whereas most spiders have eight. Also daddy longlegs produce no silk or venom, where most spiders do. For some reason many people have a certain affection for daddy longlegs, even those who claim to dislike spiders. Often a housewife who will kill a spider will carefully escort a daddy longlegs out of her house.

Daddy longlegs has a small brown body and long, thread-like legs. The two front pairs are very long allowing it to move rapidly, though awkwardly. They do not bite, but if you aren't careful in handling it, it may expel a bad odor from a pair of glands on its abdomen that is quite long lasting.

Daddy longlegs do not spin webs or make nests. They stay around loose vegetation and damp ground where there is a sup-ply of food such as small insects, spiders, and mites.

Before the first frost the female lays her eggs in a spot of damp earth where they survive the winter and hatch the following spring. Cold weather kills all the adult daddy longlegs.

98

Wolf Spider

The wolf spider is fair-sized, dark olive-brown, and hairy. It has three rows of eyes on its head, four small ones in the front row, two large ones in both the second and third rows. Its legs are strong to run down its victims. Unlike many spiders, it does not weave a web to entrap them, but pursues them on the ground.

You aren't as apt to see a wolf spider as you are some other kinds. They hunt mostly at night when the insects on which they feed are active, and when the wasps that prey on them are asleep in their nests. You may see one during the day if you turn over a stone, a piece of wood, or disturb matted grass. Wolf spiders live mostly in woods and damp fields.

The female wolf spider carries the young — sometimes as many as a hundred of them — on her back until they are old enough to fend for themselves.

Fishing Spider

With a body one-half-inch long and a leg span of up to two inches, the fishing spider is the largest spider around the Finger Lakes. It does not spin a web to trap prey, relying instead on strength, speed, and agility.

There are several species of these spiders. They can be gray, greenish-brown, yellowish-tan, or brownish-purple. You are apt to find them on a boat dock, a shoreline stone or a log near a pond, lake, stream, bog, or marsh. They are rarely found very far from water. Insects are their usual fare but they also catch small tadpoles and minnows. They lie still with legs extended until a victim gets within reach, then it is grabbed by the long legs and impaled on venomous fangs and sucked dry.

With eight large eyes and many sensory leg hairs, the fishing spider perceives the slightest movement. If approached by a large animal or a human, it hides, scooting beneath a stone, behind a tree, or down the stem of a submerged plant where it can stay underwater for up to an hour.

Late summer is the best time to look for fishing spiders. At that time the female walks on tiptoe carrying a large, round, cocoon-like egg sac. The female then builds a webbed nest by tying together the top leaves of herbaceous plants (milkweed is her favorite). Into this webbed fortress she deposits her egg sac and the emerging brood of two to three hundred spiderlings. She guards and defends the nest for about a week until the spiderlings molt their skins and drift away.

Fishing spiders are also called "nursery web" spiders.

Golden Garden Spider

Startling, because it is large, the common garden spider is one of the most beneficial, with a large web that traps a multitude of insects. Yellow and black, it usually hangs upside down in its web in plain view. This spider's web is unique with a heavy ladder-like vertical webbing in the center.

In the fall the female attaches her eggs in a cocoon-like affair to the vegetation. The spiderlings hatch in mid-winter but do not emerge until sometime in May.

JULY

The hot, hazy days of summer bring the buzz of insects. Children slog through small creeks and along lake shores, turning over stones, hoping to find some of the small creatures that hide under them. They sneak up on grasshoppers and chase butterflies; watch bumblebees sip nectar from flowers, spiders spin their webs, and dragonflies dart after mosquitoes.

The Insects

When the conversation turns to insects, many shudder thinking of creatures like flies and roaches. We may remember the itch caused by a mosquito bite, or the pain of a bee sting. There's no denying some insects are irritating, even destructive. However, we also have a myriad of beautiful butterflies and dragonflies, lady bugs, praying mantises, and fascinating oddities like the walking stick. All are insects.

Insects are the most abundant form of life. Seventy to eighty percent of all known animals are insects. There are several reasons for their proliferation. Many of them are very small, not easily seen by predators. They don't require much food and produce great numbers of young. And insects are marvelously adaptable, altering their habits to their environment. They are found in polar wastes and scorching deserts; in salt water and in fresh. They were on earth long before mammals.

An insect is distinguished from other "bugs" by a pair of antennae on its head and three pairs of legs. It has a hard outside shell or exoskeleton, divided into three sections: the head, thorax, and abdomen. Most insects go through four stages in their development: egg, larva (or nymph), pupa, and adult. With most insects, only adults have functional wings.

If it were not for insects we would not have many of the things we take for granted; honey, silk, even shellac which is the secretion of an Indian scale insect. The blossoms of most of our flowering plants would not get pollinated.

The Life of the Butterfly

Wafting on the gentle breezes of summer, butterflies are the most beautiful insects in the Finger Lakes area. The fascination with these delicate creatures is timeless. Ancient Greeks believed the soul left the body after death in the form of a butterfly; their symbol for the soul was the lovely butterfly-winged Psyche.

Butterflies' exotic colorations and patterns are created by scales, as fine as dust, that cover their wings. Some of the scales are pigmented black, brown, red, white, or yellow. Others, mostly blue and green, produce color by reflecting light from their surfaces. These often have a metallic sheen. Some naturalists think the patterns, many of which look like big eyes, may serve to scare off would-be predators. A butterfly can fall prey to a bird, lizard, frog, toad, or even a spider lying in ambush in a flower.

Most of our showier butterflies have slender, hairless, lightweight bodies and large wings. Good gliders, they can fly great distances. For flight, however, the wings must be dry, and the butterfly's body-temperature at least 86° Fahrenheit. To warm up, the insect either suns itself or shivers its wings. A butterfly rests with its wings upright.

To survive, butterflies need the nectar of flowers, and prefer those with orange or red blooms. An orange milkweed called butterfly weed that grows in our area is a particular favorite. Butterflies are least attracted to white and lavender though those are essential sources of alkaloids the males need to produce pheromones, which attracts the females for mating. Besides color, the insect looks for flowers that are upright with tubes (corollas) into which it can insert it proboscis, a long sucking tube with which it extracts the nectar. Most butterflies have taste organs on their feet. They are good pollinators.

Butterflies also require water and certain minerals and other nutrients not found in nectar but available in carrion, manure, rotting fruit, and mud puddles.

To locate a mate, a butterfly uses both sight and smell. Thousands of tiny lenses in each eye give it extraordinary vision. Its antennae are organs of smell.

Butterflies have two pairs of wings. Special scales on the wings of the males release pheromones which females can detect from quite a distance. A butterfly's antennae have little balls at the tips called clubs. During courtship the males and females circle each other touching the clubs. How this "dance" is performed varies from species to species.

The male butterfly usually dies soon after mating. The female searches for a place to lay her eggs. She may drop them at random while flying, but more often she will choose plants which will provide food for the hungry hatchlings. As the eggs are laid the female fertilizes them with the male sperm she retained in her body at the time of mating.

A butterfly begins life as a tiny egg that can range in size from almost invisible to one-tenth-inch in diameter. Most eggs are green or yellow. They can be round, oval, or cylindrical. Some are smooth; others ridged or grooved. Some hatch in a few days; others after several months. Eggs laid in the fall seldom hatch before spring.

Each egg hatches into a caterpillar, which must fend for itself. In this larval stage, which may last for two weeks, it has a voracious appetite and grows rapidly, outgrowing its skin and shedding it (molting) several times. When the caterpillar reaches its full size, it forms a hard protective shell called a chrysalis around itself. A few butterflies spin silky cocoons instead of the chrysalis. Safe in the chrysalis, or cocoon, the pupa metamorphoses and emerges as a butterfly. One hour after leaving the shell it may be ready to fly.

The lifespan of some butterflies is but a week or two. Others live up to eighteen months. Few of those that migrate to Florida or Mexico live long enough to make the return trip. However, after maturing, their offspring often continue the journey north. Longer lived butterflies that hibernate secrete a sticky liquid containing glycols related to the antifreeze used in automobiles. It hardens around them and protects them from the harshest winter cold.

Bumblebees

Nearly everyone knows what a bumblebee looks like: big, yellow and black and fuzzy; the bee whose stout, heavy body is so out of proportion with its short wings that, aerodynamically speaking, it shouldn't be able to fly at all.

There is a saying about bees, "fuzzy, friendly, smooth, scary." It's hard to imagine any bee acting affectionate, but the fuzzy bumbler comes closest. It shows aggression only when threatened. It is widely believed that if a bee — any bee — stings you, it will die immediately. This is true with some bees but not bumblebees because their stingers are not attached to their innards.

Only the queen bumblebees survive the winter, hibernating in the ground, often in a deserted mouse nest. Having mated in early fall, the queen awakens, usually in May, ready to search for a place to start a new colony of bees. Any large bumblebee you see in the spring is one of these fertile females. During the summer the smaller worker bees are out and are sometimes mistaken for bees of a different species.

The queen builds an egg cell in a hole in the soil or in a nest of dried grasses and stocks it with pollen and nectar from early spring blooms like crocus, the catkins of pussy willows, and apple blossoms. She closes the cell and then constructs a crude wax-jug about her own size and fills it with honey on which to feed during bad weather.

At this stage the queen acts more like a serf than a monarch, guarding the eggs until they hatch, then airlifting load upon load of pollen and nectar to feed the hungry larvae. Two sections on each of her hind legs are edged with long, stiff, inward-growing hairs which catch and hold the pollen as she crawls back and forth over blossoms. She works tirelessly for the ten to fourteen days it takes the larvae to reach full growth and spin their tough, paper-like cocoons in which they will pupate for one to two weeks before emerging as small adult bees.

Bees of the first brood are worker bees, sterile females. Now the queen, who will devote the rest of her life to egg laying, is treated like royalty. The workers immediately begin their duties, feeding her and laying up a small store of honey for cold or wet weather when they are unable to fly. For bees, flight is impossible when they are wet and/or cold. Sometimes a bumblebee afield after sundown will cling, benumbed, to a blossom until afternoon of the next day when its body warms up enough to permit movement.

The queen lays more eggs; the workers tend them. With more bees to tend them, each succeeding hatch is larger than the earlier ones. Thus the colony grows.

By late summer a few fertile females hatch from special eggs. Then a batch of males, or drones, emerges. They mate and the females become the young queens who will spend the winter in hibernation, awaking in the spring to start another cycle. Any bumblebees you see in early fall are these queens searching for places to hibernate.

During a mid-winter thaw if the temperature gets high enough, a queen may venture from her hiding place only to die when the temperature drops suddenly, she becomes confused and can't find her original shelter and hastily takes whatever is at hand, however unsuitable.

Grasshoppers

Probably every child who has ever spent a summer in the country around the Finger Lakes has chased after a grasshopper only to have it jump away at the expected moment of capture. It can leap a considerable distance for its legs are extraordinarily powerful. Relative to its size, a grasshopper has 120 times the kicking power of the average man.

But it isn't only children who pursue grasshoppers. Fishermen catch them to use as bait for several species of game fish.

Grasshoppers mate in the fall. The female lays her eggs in the ground by inserting her ovipositor about one inch beneath the surface. She covers the eggs with a thick secretion which holds them together in pods and which protects them from either too much or too little rain.

Grasshoppers are one of several insects that reach adulthood in but three stages. The young nymphs appear anywhere from May to July. White at birth, in a few hours they will have taken on the green coloration of the adult species. They undergo several molts during the forty to sixty days it takes them to reach adulthood and become capable of flight though they are not considered real flying insects as they do not have wings.

Spiders find grasshoppers a tasty meal as do most birds.

The depredations of grasshoppers in America's breadbasket are well documented. In our area, however, there is only one generation of them per year, and they seldom do serious damage.

The Moths

There are between 700 and 800 species of butterflies in North America outside Mexico, but there are ten times that number of moths.

The life history of moths is almost the same as those of butterflies. The eggs of both, which the females lay in great numbers, hatch into larvae or caterpillars, which crawl about plants and feed on the leaves. They molt several times.

When they reach the pupal stage, however, you begin to see differences. Moths spin grey soft cocoons in which to pupate. Some moth larvae burrow into the ground or under a stone for shelter. Nearly all butterflies form hard chrysalises which are often shiny and colorful.

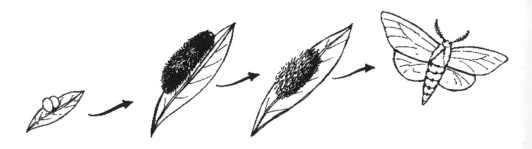

Moth antennae are not clubbed on the ends like those of butterflies but shaped like tiny feathers. Moths have, however, "scale wings" like butterflies. Their legs also have scales on the lower parts and long silky hairs on the uppers.

For sheer beauty some of the big moths rival the butterflies, though because they fly at night, they are not often seen.

Moths are more apt to light on you than butterflies, and when they do, they feel hairy. Butterflies perch with wings upright, moths with wings spread flat. Like many creatures of the night, moths are a little mysterious and can be startling if one lands on you unexpectedly. However, if you can bring them into your environment, you will soon see how fascinating they are.

To attract moths, try "sugaring." Mix about four pounds of sugar with a bottle of stale beer and about one-half cup of rum, either dark or light. Moths aren't brand loyal so the cheapest you can get is just fine with them.

Moths are most active on hot, humid, moonless nights just before a thunderstorm, right after a rain, or on a night when the moon shines brightly.

Polyphemus Moth

With a five-inch wingspread, olive colored and handsomely marked, the Polyphemus moth is a magnificent insect. Because it has two black-rimmed yellow and blue spots which look like protruding eyeballs on its hindwings, and two smaller "eyes" on its forewings, it was named for the one-eyed giant Polyphemus, who was blinded by Ulysses on the way back from Troy to his own kingdom of Ithaca. The Polyphemus does not, however, resemble its namesake of which Virgil wrote, "A horrible monster, misshapen, vast."

Unlike most moths which sip the nectar of flowers, the adult Polyphemus does not feed at all but lives on the fat stored within its body. The insect's adult life is so short the female barely has time to mate and lay her bun-shaped eggs in clusters on leaves, usually those of birch, chestnut, maple, or wild rose. Often the female Polyphemus dies so soon after egg laying she falls to the ground under the host plant that will nourish the next generation. In the Finger Lakes, there is but one brood each year.

The Polyphemus larva has an enormous appetite. It spends

fifty-six days as a caterpillar, green segmented, with red and white markings; knobbed and bristled like the larvae of most butterflies and moths. They have developed these unique characteristics to help ward off predators, especially birds.

After its last molt the Polyphemus caterpillar is ready to spin its cocoon. The silk it uses is not a continuous thread and cannot be unreeled. It is of greater density than that of most other moths. Once spinning is completed, the cocoon's fibers are permeated by a fluid released by the caterpillar. Either fastened to a twig or rolled up in leaves, the dried chalk-white cocoon is the caterpillar's winter home. The moth emerges in May or June.

Cecropia Moth

The striking Cecropia is the largest moth in North America north of Mexico. The Cecropia is very common in the Finger Lakes Region. The largest specimens have a wing expanse of seven inches.

The Cecropia's body is a stout and fuzzy and dark red with white stripes across its abdomen. Its wings are a soft olive green, dull red near the bases, the outer edges of which are banded in shades of white and red. Near the center of each wing is a whitish crescent-shaped spot. Unfortunately, because it flies at night, the extraordinary beauty of the Cecropia is rarely seen.

The Cecropia caterpillar, which grows to a length of four inches, is blue-green with yellow, red, and blue knobs, and black bristles. It feeds on a variety of plants. Elderberry is its favorite.

The cocoon of the pupating insect is distinctive. Often as much as three inches long, you will find it securely fastened along its entire length to a twig or branch.

Tomato Hornworm Moth

We have two common sphinx moths in our area. One, the Tomato Hornworm, has a fuzzy green and red body and wings with a wide margin of red.

As you watch one of these thick-bodied insects hovering over a blossom at dusk, probing deep into the bloom with its remarkably long proboscis, you can easily mistake it for a hummingbird. As an adult, it too feeds on nectar.

Most gardeners are familiar with this moth's larva: the large, fat, horned, garishly marked tomato worm. With a voracious appetite, one can completely destroy a tomato plant in short order.

White-lined Sphinx Moth

The white-lined sphinx flies during the day, especially when it is cloudy, as well as at night, and from June until the cold weather sets in. It is widely distributed throughout the Finger Lakes area.

Like all sphinx moths, it has a thick, bullet-shaped body, long narrow forewings, small hindwings, and large eyes. The veins of its beige forewings are edged with white, and a pinkish band reaches from the apex to the base.

A wide reddish band crosses each dark brown rear wing. Its wing expanse is about four inches.

If you disturb a white-lined sphinx when it is resting—perhaps among the branches of a small, dense evergreen tree—it will vibrate its wings rapidly for a minute or more to raise its internal temperature enough to fly, sort of like revving up its engine.

White-lined sphinx larvae feed on many kinds of plants including grape, apple, Virginia creeper, and currant.

Sphinx moths are fast fliers, perhaps that is why they are often mistaken for birds. They have been recorded at up to thirty-three-miles-per-hour.

Crayfish

Children around the Finger Lakes spend many happy summer hours slogging in small streams, turning over rocks and debris in pursuit of crayfish. The fresh water version of the lobster, these small creatures have front claws and the youngsters soon learn to grasp them around their middles to avoid being pinched.

Crayfish are extremely wary and can scuttle away in a flash. Greenish or brownish-olive, they are nocturnal feeders, scavengers that feed on plant and animal debris and help to keep our streams clean. They also eat worms, snails, and insect larvae. In turn, crayfish are eaten by turtles, snakes, frogs, water birds, fish, raccoons, and humans. They are tasty morsels. Fishermen also use them as bait for bass, yellow perch, catfish, pickerel, and walleyes.

Crayfish measure three to six inches long. Egg laying occurs from March to June. The young mature in two years, and live, on average, four to six years.

Crayfish are also known as Ditch Bugs, Mud-bugs, crawdads, and crawfish.

112

Mudpuppy

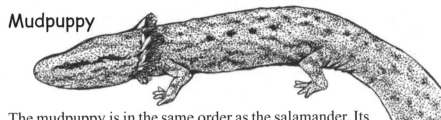

The mudpuppy is in the same order as the salamander. Its
unusual name comes from the fact that when it is taken out of
the water, it sometimes makes a sound like the whine of a puppy.
Mainly nocturnal, during the day it hides under stones or buried in
the mud of lakes, ponds, and rivers. Therefore, it is most often found
by accident. I have seen them in both Seneca and Cayuga Lakes in the
Finger Lakes region.

Gray or dark brown with indistinct bluish-black mottling, a squarish-
flat head with small eyes, slow, sluggish, and slippery, it is attractive only
to another mudpuppy. Poison glands in its skin ward off most predators,
however, the poison is not strong enough to affect humans. A mudpuppy can
grow up to two feet in length, but most are about half that size. Each foot has
four fairly long toes.

Worms, insect larvae, fish eggs, crayfish, and frogs' eggs are their diet.

Mudpuppies mate just before entering their dormant winter state. A pair
may share the same winter hole in a bank. In the spring the female lays from
eighteen to eight hundred yellowish eggs, each approximately one-quarter of
an inch across and encased in its own jelly envelope. The female then buries them individually in a crowded mass on the underside of a log or large
stone, occasionally in a sandy hollow on a streambed. The water temperature
determines how long it will take them to hatch — it can be anywhere from
thirty-eight-to-sixty-three days — during which time the female guards the
nest.

The young hatch with the yolk sac hanging from their abdomens. It will
be their food supply for about two months or until they are one and one-half
inches long.

Mudpuppies mature at between five and seven years when they are about
eight inches long. It is believed they may live for up to twenty years.

AUGUST

By the time August rolls around, there is a noticeable shortening of days around the Finger Lakes. Bats stream from their daytime roosts a little earlier to go on their nocturnal hunts. The evening symphony of nature tunes up: crickets, tree crickets, katydids, and cicadas, while birds all but cease their singing as those that migrate begin to flock for the journey south. Animals begin to prepare for winter, each species in its own fashion. But large, beautiful moths still fly to outside lights.

Bats Give Birth

The most common species of bats found around the Finger Lakes are the little brown with a six-inch wingspan, the larger big brown, the silver-haired, the red, and the hoary, all descriptive names.

Bats are nocturnal. In the deepening twilight of late spring and summer thousands of them pour out of their caves, attics, barns, or mines and fan out through the countryside. You see them flying erratically along lake shores, around streams and ponds or wherever insects are plentiful. Actually, bats are of great benefit to humans because of their tremendous appetite for insects. Mosquitoes are their principal food.

Like most wild creatures bats should not be disturbed. They will bite if angered or frightened, and can carry the rabies virus.

Bats are the only mammals capable of true flight. Their forelegs are webbed wings which have the same skeletal elements as the human arm with the bones in the widely separated fingers greatly elongated.

Many years ago scientists discovered that bats have a built-in sonar system that enables them to fly in the dark and avoid bumping into obstructions. In flight they emit high frequency sounds inaudible to the human ear that bounce off objects and back to the bat. Amazingly, the bat can home in on insects but avoid other objects. This ability is called "echolocation."

Bats mate in the fall but do not give birth until late spring. The babies live on their mothers' milk until they are able to fly. They are prolific, ranking second only to rodents in numbers.

Between May and July, female bats gather in colonies of one hundred or more in dark hiding places. They drive away all the males and then give birth to naked, pink, blind babies. The young reach full size and can fly when they are three weeks old. Soon they are flying at full speed, mouths open to scoop up insects.

A bat lives an average of three to four years, though banded specimens that are ten-to-twelve-years-old have been found. The species have been around a very long time. Fossil remains have been found in rocks over fifty million years old. They are secretive and since early times they have been objects of fear, folklore, and superstition.

Some bats migrate while others over-winter in caves and abandoned mines.

Owls are about the bats' only enemies.

In the last few years many people have lost some of their fear and aversion to bats. Some of them are even putting up bat houses like many of us do bird houses.

Crickets

When warm weather settles in, the field cricket's cheerful "chirrup, chirrup" mingles with the stridulated fiddling of the tree crickets to fill the dusk with bewitching music. If you lay your head back and close your eyes, it is quite easy to conjure up an image of Jiminy Cricket dancing debonairly from twig to twig.

In our area, field crickets are the most common species, abounding in lawns and fields close to the soil. Shiny dark brown or black insects, the male measures about one inch in length with the female somewhat longer. Solitary creatures, they are reclusive, and retreat when approached. If forced to travel, they jump with their powerful hind legs. Their tiny wings, which lie under their wing covers, are too feeble for flight.

Only the males sing, and their singing serves two purposes: to stake out a territory and to attract a mate. Scientists haven't determined the exact area of a cricket's territory. However, by recording one male's voice and playing it close to another caged male, one naturalist found that playing the recording nearer than two feet to the imprisoned male made him go wild and attack the screened walls of his cage.

During mating season, male crickets become very combative. In early China, cricket fights were a popular spectator sport. Victorious fighters were very valuable—worth $100 each. Upon death, one would be placed in a tiny silver coffin and buried with great solemnity.

For his den, the male field cricket selects a tiny hole in the ground, a crack in a wall, or a crevice under a piece of bark. From this bastion, he lifts his wing covers and rubs the "scraper" on the underside of one against the "file" on the underside of the other to produce the distinctive cricket "song."

Unlike many insects, sexing a cricket is easy. At his rear, the male has two thin, prong-like sensory organs. The female has three. The spear-like, longer middle one is the ovipositor with which she injects her eggs into the soil.

Each female lays several hundred eggs. They hatch in May or June, and thousands of the young crick-ets, called nymphs, swarm through the tall grass. They resemble the adults except they lack wings. In crickets there is no pupal state. The nymphs soon molt and their skin hardens. By late July or early August they are ready to "sing." It isn't easy to pinpoint the exact location of a chirping cricket. When you approach him, he is quiet.

All field crickets hear one another's song through ears which are located on one of their legs just under the "knee." Their calls vary in intensity. The louder the call, the more attractive to the females. However, it is not unusual for a silent male to "steal" a female on her way to a calling male. At sunrise, both males and females gather under dense vegetation to avoid being eaten by waking birds.

Scavenging through the darkness for tiny insects, a cricket can end up as an hors d'oeuvre for a skunk or the main dish for a toad. They aren't exactly a protected species in the daytime either. One September I saw one being devoured by a praying mantis.

Crickets can bite. They also can become tame and tolerate human com-pany. People like crickets too, perhaps because they have been considered good luck symbols. In the Orient, crickets were once prized for their songs and kept as pets. They were housed in elaborately carved cages of ivory and jade—peasants housed theirs in bamboo cages. At one time, in Japanese homes, crickets were kept to warn of intruders. Today a tiny cricket cage is a much-sought-after antique.

You can still keep a cricket as a pet. It requires only food and water, and will eat almost anything—apple peelings, sunflower seeds, dry dog food—but not much of it. If it gets loose in your house, it will snack on your woolens.

A pet cricket will not live very long. It would be most unlikely for one to survive beyond the late Fall.

Tree Crickets

While field crickets chirp from their lairs on the ground; tree crickets shrill from trees and bushes. Pale apple-green or white tinged with green—occasionally brown, they have been called the blondes of the cricket family. They are a little larger than their field cousins.

Only the males of the species hear each others' songs; the females are deaf. The female "hears" by smelling the air with her long, sensitive antennae. When the male elevates his wings to sing, a gland on his back is exposed. The odor from this gland attracts the female who runs to the male and nibbles at the fluid from the gland.

Like field crickets, tree crickets lay their eggs in the fall. They puncture holes through the bark of twigs, and deposit their eggs. A particularly heavy cricket population can cause damage to trees and berry bushes because the punctures make it possible for fungus infections to get in.

Even a slight change in the weather affects the sensitive crickets. Farmers once believed them to be infallible weather forecasters. If the cricket's chirping continued until late in the evening, they didn't worry about frost. However, when the cricket's evening song waned, they covered their tomatoes, and kept the cat in for the night.

In 1897, A.E. Dolbear, a physics professor at Tufts University, noticed that tree crickets chirp faster as the temperature rises. Accordingly, he came up with a formula for telling the temperature: count the number of chirps in fifteen seconds and add forty.

A cricket's happy fiddling ceases at first frost, when he drags himself away to die or, sometimes, to dig a burrow with a small chamber at the inner end, where he will spend the winter in hibernation.

The Cyclical Cicada

The seventeen-year, or periodical, cicada is the Rip van Winkle of the insect family. Because these insects are on a seventeen-year cycle, you might think you can see them only every seventeen years. However, all of them are not on the same year's cycle so you see some every summer. Nevertheless, where there is a heavy concentration of them one year you can expect to see great numbers of them at the same place seventeen years later. In 1984 there was a banner year for cicadas in several locations around the Finger Lakes. Years and dates of their expected appearance can be obtained in advance from New York State experiment stations.

Often incorrectly called seventeen-year locusts (both belong to the grasshopper family), swarms of which can cause immense damage to crops in America's heartland, cicadas are extremely slow growing with very dainty appetites. However, young orchard trees, forests, and ornamentals can suffer damage in years of heavy population by the females, which make many incisions in the bark during egg laying.

In late summer the female cicada lays her 200 to 600 eggs in row upon row of pockets she cuts in twigs using her

119

tough ovipositor. In six to seven weeks the eggs hatch. The nymphs fall to the ground where they burrow down and attach themselves to the rootlets. Their first seventeen years are spent in darkness underground where, as a pupae, they cling to rootlets and suck the tree's juices.

They emerge to spend their five-week adult lifespan. Their skins split open and the mature insects emerge. They rest briefly while their wings dry out in preparation for flight. You often see their brown shed skins clinging to the bark of trees. The adults are also good jumpers. With the possible exception of the termite queen, no other insect is known to live longer.

Cicadas are about two inches long, greenish marked with red and black. They have four membranous wings, prominent eyes in a wide head, and abdomens of six sections.

You probably will hear more cicadas than you will ever see. Night singers, they are considered predictors of hot weather perhaps because you don't hear them until summer is well advanced. As is the case with most insects, only the male cicada "sings." His musical equipment is probably the most complicated in the insect world: drum-like membranes within two concealed cavities which he vibrates rapidly with seemingly tireless muscles. His "song" is not melodic but rather a loud insistent buzz.

In other cultures singing insects have been held in high esteem. In Japan, night singers were more valued than those of day, and centuries ago the Greeks kept cicadas in cages, gave them as prestigious gifts, and put charming epitaphs on graves of favorites.

Cicadas have one serious natural enemy: the large, blue-black cicada killer wasp. This wasp, which lives in holes in the earth, does not actually kill the cicada. Its sting stuns it so the wasp can carry it to its underground home where the cicada becomes food for a young wasp-to-be. The female wasp lays her egg in the hole. When one cicada is buried a male wasp hatches; when two are buried in the same hole, a female.

The young wasp completes feeding during the fall, but spends the winter in the pupal stage in the same hole. In the spring it crawls out, becomes an adult wasp and goes looking for a hapless cicada.

The Call of the Katydid

Katydids are easily identified by their calls. From about the tenth of August, like town criers, throughout late summer nights they loudly proclaim their presence throughout the Finger Lakes

Only the male "sings." To attract a mate he rubs a scraper at the base of one of his front wings across a file at the base of the other. The call can carry as far as a quarter of a mile through a still summer night.

You are much more apt to hear katydids than you are to see them. A vibrant, green color, they blend with the leaves on which they dwell. Rarely, a brown or pink specimen is found.

A full-grown katydid is about one and one-half to two inches long. They are graceful, oval-winged creatures with broad, boat-shaped bodies. Their wing covers are thin and delicate; their two antennae upon their heads long and fragile. They are not fond of being handled and can deal a sharp, but not poisonous, nip.

Katydids belong to the same family as crickets, grasshoppers, and cockroaches, and like their grasshopper relatives, are good jumpers. Though they feed on leaves and tender twigs, unlike grasshoppers, they are relatively harmless to vegetation.

In early fall each female lays two hundred or more slate-colored, oval-shaped, flat eggs, each about one-eighth-inch long, in overlapping rows on twigs and leaves. She secretes a glue that holds the eggs in place.

With autumn frosts, the final curtain falls on the katydid chorus. Some old timers claim the first frost will occur six weeks after you hear the first katydid.

In the spring the tops of the eggs laid the previous fall crack open and the tiny

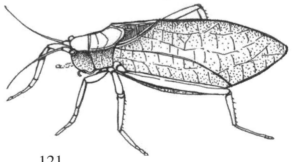

young wingless "katys" wriggle out. Upon emerging they are pale but soon assume the leaf-green color of the adults. In our area there is but one brood a year. The adult katydids do not live through the winter.

Salamanders

Salamanders are amphibians, like frogs and toads, but are sometimes mistaken for lizards because of their long tails. However, there is an obvious distinction. Lizards are reptiles and are covered with dry scales while salamanders have smooth, moist skin. On land salamanders always seek damp, shady places because they will die if their skins dry out.

Basically voiceless with elongate bodies, long tapering tails, and four widely-separated legs that project from the sides of their bodies, salamanders absorb water and air through their skin as well as their lungs or gills. Most of them lead a double life, one aquatic and the other terrestrial.

Red-spotted Salamander (Red eft)

The red-spotted salamander begins life in the water where it hatches from an egg. The newt, or eft, is less than a quarter of an inch long with feathery gills almost as long as its body. It spends its first summer in the water as a dull green larva.

Sometime between August and October it puts on an orange coat with two rows of black-bordered red spots, absorbs its gills, develops lungs and legs, and crawls out of the water to live in the woods. In this phase it is called a red newt. Two to three inches long, it will remain terrestrial for about three years. Diurnal, it is out mostly on cloudy or rainy days eating tiny snails, insects and their larvae, worms and spiders. It spends the winter under stones and logs, sometimes burrowing a few inches into the soil.

Because of its bright color one might think the red newt would be easy prey for hungry predators. Instead, the color serves as a warning to them. There is a powerful neurotoxin in its skin glands, harmless to humans but not to would-be predators.

As the newt approaches maturity it is about four inches long and gradually turns olive-colored. Its skin becomes slippery and fins develop above and below the tail. Black spots appear on its orange belly. When fully matured it goes back to the water to breed. It looks so different from the red eft stage, it is often mistaken for a different species. However, the identifying spots are always there.

The adult red-spotted salamander spends the rest of its life in the water but it must surface to breathe. It's a friend to humans because it consumes great quantities of mosquito larvae. It also eats grubs, mollusks, frogs' eggs, insect larvae, and the eggs of other salamanders.

The adult male develops rough black patches along the undersides of his strong hindlegs, which he uses to clasp the female when mating. A pair may remain locked together for as long as ten minutes almost motionless. Then the excited male twists and shakes the female, stimulating her to ovulation. He then releases her and deposits several clusters of sperm cells, which she walks over and picks up, with the lips of her cloaca. Thus the eggs are fertilized internally.

A short time later the female deposits 200 to 400 eggs, each inside its own gelatinous sack. She sticks each sac singly to twigs or aquatic vegetation near the bottom of a pond where they are effectively concealed. Depending on the temperature of the water, the eggs will hatch in two to four weeks.

Tiger Salamander

The adult tiger salamander is about seven inches long with a heavy black body splashed with yellow. It begins life in water but as an adult is terrestrial.

Found only in eastern North America, it is on New York State's endangered species list. Although they are relatively rare to spot, you are certain to find them in the Finger Lakes Region.

Yellow-spotted Salamander

Unlike the red-spotted, the shiny, yellow-spotted salamander spends its life on land, returning in the spring to lay its eggs in the water. It is smaller — about six inches long — and slimmer than the tiger salamander; its spots rounder.

SEPTEMBER

September is a transitional month around the Finger Lakes. The autumnal equinox, falling around the twentieth, spells the end of summer. Birdsong is replaced with the honking of Canada geese; the monarch butterflies mass and begin their migration to Mexico. Wooly bear caterpillars are crawling about, and those who think they are weather prognosticators are examining them to see if the winter will be mild or severe.

Giant Puffballs

You can't mistake a giant puffball for anything else. White, spherical, and commonly a foot in diameter, they usually grow in wooded areas, lawns, or fields. They propagate by dissemination of their spores by the wind. They pop up in late September after cool fall rains and tend to reoccur in the same places year after year.

Giant puffballs are good and safe to eat. Sliced and fried in butter, they taste much like mushrooms. While you can eat giant puffballs with impunity, you should never eat wild mushrooms unless you know what you are doing. Some are harmless but others are so poisonous one small bite can kill you.

Giant puffballs grow fast and must be used as soon as they are large enough. Once they reach maturity they deteriorate rapidly, becoming brown and eventually, powdery.

The Squirrels — Gray Squirrels

There are many nut and seed bearing trees around the Finger Lakes, therefore, there are also many squirrels. Grays, with slender bodies measuring ten or so inches and a big bushy tail about as long, are the largest. Bright-eyed and graceful, they leap from branch to branch, frisk up and down trees and dance along electric wires.

In the wild, gray squirrels spend most of the time in trees, eating seeds from pine-cones, nuts, berries and fruit. They come down only to bury their larder. Those that live around people, however, spend more time on the ground, often raiding bird feeders. Though capable pantry stockers, they quickly get used to the easy life. Some bird lovers don't mind as they enjoy watching squirrels as well as birds. Others get squirrel-proof feeders.

If you have nut trees in your yard, you will have lots of squirrels. One fall afternoon I watched a pair of them scramble up a big black walnut tree, bite off several nuts, scoot back down and carry them away, one at a time, to be buried. Watching them I could well understand how the expression "to squirrel away" came about.

In the spring I've seen squirrels dig up butternuts buried the previous fall only to rebury them not more than a foot away.

Until recently naturalists didn't know how a squirrel identified the nuts it had buried months earlier, so they conducted an experiment. They put several of the animals in an enclosed area along with a bunch of nuts. After the squirrels had buried them, the wildlife biologists dug up some of the nuts and reburied them in different locations. Upon being returned to the area, each squirrel dug where it had buried its nuts, even in the places from which the biologists had removed them. Therefore, the scientists determined the animals relied on memory, not scent or some other factor, to find their food supply.

Gray squirrels build nests of leaves high in the branches of trees. They mate in January or February. After a forty-four-day gestation period the female gives birth to two to three blind, naked babies. At the end of two months they are weaned. There is a second litter in July or August.

If the mother squirrel moves her young, she holds the infant in her mouth by its stomach while it curls its head and tail around her face.

Gray squirrels are good reforestation animals. They bury each nut or acorn in a separate small hole. Those that are not recovered sprout to become future trees.

Their extraordinary quickness and agility enable squirrels to elude most would-be ground predators, but one sometimes falls victim to a hungry hawk or owl.

Red Squirrels

Red squirrels are reddish-brown in color with white undersides. They are like the grays in many respects, but are much smaller and less tame. Both eat nuts, seeds, and acorns, but red squirrels are more aggressive and will raid birds' nests and devour the eggs and young. The red squirrel's diet also includes seeds found in evergreen cones, so large numbers of red squirrels are found in stands of conifers. People whose homes are surrounded by mature evergreens often have problems with red squirrels chewing into their attics. They also can damage unattended cabins.

Diurnal and active all year, red squirrels will tunnel under the snow to reach their caches. Unlike grays, they stockpile spruce and pine cones, seeds, acorns, and nuts in one spot. They often have a favorite feeding stump under which you find big piles of cone husks or nutshells.

Red squirrels live in tree cavities, but often build nests, if cavities are not available. They raise two broods of from four or more a year, one in April or May, the other in August or September.

Territorial and feisty, these little animals will chase the much larger gray squirrels out of an area. It's quite likely you will hear a red squirrel before you see it. Sitting on a branch ten or twenty feet up in a tree, it scolds raucously.

If it manages to evade birds of prey, a red squirrel can live up to ten years.

The Solitary Chipmunk

The little chipmunk entertains campers and picnickers all around the Finger Lakes, scampering about with its tail held straight up.

With a five to six-inch body and a three to four-inch tail, Chipmunks have light cream colored facial stripes above and below their eyes. Golden brown, it also has black-bordered, white stripes on its sides and back which end at its reddish rump. Its front and underside are a light buff. A rodent like its larger, relative, the squirrel, it has a much less bushy tail.

Chipmunks are found in deciduous woodland's and brushy areas where they feed on nuts, seeds, roots, insects, birds' eggs, and fruit. They will also dig up and eat tulip and other flowering bulbs. Like raccoons, they have a fondness for corn and will climb a stalk, sit on top of the ear and nibble the kernels. As cute as they are, they can do considerable damage.

Though they can climb trees, you find these little animals mostly on the ground. They nest and spend the winter in extensive underground burrows. A chipmunk digs constantly, extending tunnels and opening new storage chambers while closing the original opening where a pile of dirt has accumulated. Its active entrances are plunge holes around which there are no signs of ground disturbance. The main chamber can be up to a cubic foot in size with two or three others farther down the tunnel. The chipmunk builds a small chamber at the lowest point in the tunnel system to use for excrement.

Except for a mother with her young, chipmunks lead solitary lives. They spend much of the summer and early fall laying in their winter food supply, which they carry to their burrows in their cheek pouches.

A few days of below fifty degree temperatures send the chipmunk below ground to sleep the winter away. Not a true hibernator, it wakes up periodically and drags out some of its stored provisions for a snack. On warm winter days it may even poke its head up through the snow.

In the wild chipmunks live three years or more. They breed the first year. The first litter of four or five is born in May and the second in August or September. The young appear above ground when two-thirds grown.

Fall Migration

Migration may be the least understood of all bird behavior. After much study, scientists don't know for sure what triggers it. They theorize the birds may be able to sense changes in barometric pressure associated with storm front movements. Some think the birds may be able to hear infrasonic waves. No one knows what keeps them on course. Do they navigate by the stars? The earth's magnetic fields? Landmarks?

The bobolink makes the longest migration of any New World land bird, flying from Canada and northern New York — including the Finger Lakes—to northern Argentina and Chile. Researchers at the State University of New York at Geneseo found that a bobolink's body contains iron oxide, and think it may indicate a compass connection.

The exodus of songbirds from the Finger Lakes begins in mid-September. The departure of waterfowl is heralded by the honking of the Canada geese flying in their characteristic V formations. However, thousands of the geese winter over at the north end of Cayuga Lake. Sometimes individuals of other normally migratory species spend all winter along with the permanent residents: chickadees, nuthatches, cardinals, tufted titmice, blue jays, most woodpeckers, and some hawks. Bird feeders often supply enough food to sustain the birds throughout the usually scarce winter months.

During the winter months, rafts of ducks of different species can be seen on the big unfrozen Finger Lakes. Birders believe this is because they feel safer from land predators here.

The Praying Mantis

The praying mantis is not a native of the Finger Lakes area. It was imported into the United States from China during the last half of the 1800s.

A handsome mix of greens and browns, a mantis blends perfectly with twigs, grasses, and other vegetation. It has a long, curving abdomen topped by a pair of folded gossamer wings. Its small thorax is cropped by a large, metallic-green, pointed head with two large bulging eyes made up of hundreds of facets.

Female mantis rarely fly. The smaller, lighter males, however, often take to the air in search of females. In early autumn they mate and the female lays her eggs in a thick, creamy substance which she secretes, then whips into foam with two whirling appendages at the tip of her abdomen. The foam soon hardens, sealing the eggs in a protective, insulated case where they will spend the winter. Each case, which contains fifty to one hundred eggs, is attached to trees and shrubs, near to the ground.

The cocoons warm and soften in the spring sunshine. Thousands of tiny mantids crawl from the cases through tunnels leading from the central chamber. They look like miniature adults except they have no wings.

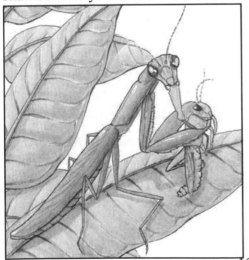

At this stage they are vulnerable to ants which kill and carry off as many of them as possible. Apparently mantis have a genetic memory for they have a lifetime dread of ants. They are the only creatures from which a mantis will back down.

For its size the mantis just may have the most ravenous appetite of any creature on earth. The female is larger than the male, more powerful and more deadly; a master executioner. After mating, she usually eats her mate and sometimes her young. Among mantises, cannibalism is common from birth to death.

Young mantises which escape ants, their parents, and siblings scoot off and set up kingdoms of their own.

Vicious fights between female mantis are common. They fight to the death, stalking, parrying, lunging and striking at each other's heads until one manages to behead its opponent. At one time in China mantis fights were staged sporting events.

These antisocial predators are not easily intimidated, even by humans. If one sees you watching it, it will fix you with an icy stare, turning its head to follow your movements. It is the only insect that can turn its head from side to side.

When stalking its prey, the mantis' large eyes give it the ability to see the precise location of its victim before it strikes. It moves slowly and stealthily. When ready to strike, however, it does a complete turnaround, suddenly lowering its large forelegs, which are lined with deadly spines. The scythe-shaped claws at the tops of them hook and immobilize the prey. In a split second it is all over.

A mantis eats only live prey, not bothering to kill it prior to dining. Holding the wriggling victim between its formidable forearms, it feasts leisurely.

Mantids are preyed upon by spiders, birds, and small mammals. However, they are so fierce and fearless, and put up such tremendous battles, they often end up as victors instead of victims. Also, when threatened or annoyed they spit a sour brown liquid.

Like a small child about to say grace, hands clasped beneath its bowed head, the praying mantis sits motionless on a stem. If it is praying at all, it is for the speedy delivery of its next meal. Perhaps a better name for this insect would be "preying" mantis.

A praying mantis is a gardener's friend, eating many insects harmful to garden vegetation. Seed houses sell their egg cases as an aid to organic agriculture.

Isabella Tiger Moth

When you see the familiar wooly bear caterpillar, that supposed predictor of winter weather, you are looking at a future Isabella Tiger Moth. When it crawls about in the fall it is looking for a protected place to curl up and spend the winter where it will remain dormant until the spring sun warms the earth.

In the spring the caterpillar crawls about searching for its first meal of plantain. Any variety of the plant is acceptable. It gorges for a time, then fasts and ceases all movement. Suddenly it springs to life again and goes looking for a place to pupate, such as on old boards, the undersides of stones or some other spot.

The caterpillar spins a thread from its silk-producing glands and hair and weaves it into a cocoon, which it spins about itself. In about two weeks the cocoon splits and the Isabella Tiger Moth emerges. It is light brown and has a wingspread of about two inches.

Immediately after mating, the female lays up to a thousand round, yellow eggs in small clusters on some species of plantain. After hatching, the larvae eat, grow, and molt. By fall they are full-grown caterpillars and the process begins again.

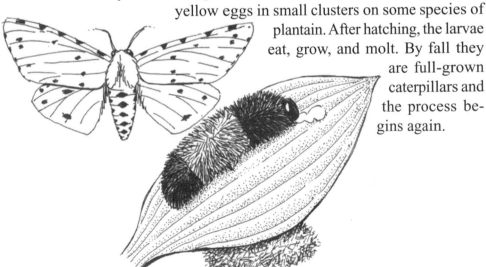

133

A Royal Beauty

You can't miss the monarch. It is the most common large butterfly in the Finger Lakes Region; the one with orange, black-veined wings bordered with a black band sprinkled with white spots; the one that sails languidly beside the road or perches on a flower.

Monarchs are unique among butterflies in their migration. Leaving the Finger Lakes in mid-September, they travel in groups of thousands the many miles across the United States to spend the winter in Mexico. Sometimes, toward evening you can see masses of them clinging to the lower branches of evergreen trees along the shores of lakes. Unfortunately, you can also see many that have been killed on the highways.

In late April or early May they return, but not en masse. Their northern arrival is protracted and individual.

Several generations of monarchs are born, breed, and die during their long journeys back and forth. The progeny continue on in the same direction though they have no knowledge of the route or direction. Lepidopterists (butterfly specialists) aren't sure how this happens. They speculate it is genetic programming but concede it also could be the magnetic field, some low-frequency sound, star patterns, or even odors from evergreens.

Another peculiarity for which naturalists have not established a reason is the butterfly's special aversion to the ruby-throated hummingbird. A monarch will harass one of the birds at a feeder until it flies away.

Monarch larvae feed only on milkweed. Therefore, the female lays her ridged, loaf-shaped green eggs on some species of that plant. Within a week the hatchlings wriggle out and begin feeding.

The white milkweed sap contains noxious alkaloids poisonous to most other insects. The brightly colored, black-striped monarch caterpillar, however, laps it up, and separates out and stores the foul-smelling alkaloids for self-defense. The alkaloids are what make both the caterpillar and the adult butterfly extremely nauseating to predators.

As the larvae grow they shed their skin. Their first molt occurs in about two days. During their eleven days of growth they molt three more times. The full-grown caterpillar then encases itself inside a greenish, iridescent chrysalis. It can take from two weeks to several months for the larva to transform or metamorphose into a butterfly. For some days before emergence you can see wing patterns through the shell of the chrysalis.

Upon squeezing out of its shell, the monarch has a fat body and flaccid wings. As it pumps up its stored body fluid into the wings, they take shape and the body shrinks.

The adult monarch fuels up on nectar for the energy to exist, breed, and migrate. It sips from many species of flowers, besides milkweed. It particularly savors red clover. With a sense of taste 1,400 times greater than that of humans, a monarch can detect the most minute sugar content in a flower. In late summer monarchs sip from goldenrod blossoms.

The Viceroy

Though it is a darker orange and smaller (under three inches), at first glance the viceroy can be mistaken for a monarch. Therefore, it is seldom attacked by predators though it has no defensive poisonous alkaloids.

The viceroy flies somewhat faster than the monarch, with flapping alternating with glides, wings held horizontally. The monarch holds its wings slanted upward. The viceroy also has heavier black along the veins. The absolute distinguishing mark is a black post-median line across its hind wings.

Very common throughout the Finger Lakes area, it likes open spaces, meadows, and roadsides. It is very fond of flowers and the juices of fungi on decaying wood.

The viceroy caterpillar is unique. It has a brown segmented body with a greenish head and two horns. Feeding mostly at night, by day it rests on twigs or the exposed midribs of chewed leaves such as willow, poplar, aspen, plum, cherry, and apple. When partly grown, it hibernates in a tube made of the rolled-up basal part of a leaf that is fastened to the twig of the food plant, exposed to every kind of winter weather. The adult butterfly appears in late May or early June.

OCTOBER

In the Finger Lakes region the month of October is heralded for its "bright blue weather." It's also known as the month when the deciduous trees emblazon our countryside. It often brings the first light snowfall which usually disappears within hours. The deep sleepers of the area, particularly the woodchuck and the black bear, are gorging themselves to put on enough fat to survive the long fast ahead. Many of the smaller mammals are adding to their winter cache. For people, the pleasantly cool weather and most of the biting insects are already in hibernation or killed off by the cold, it's a great time for walks in the country.

Fall Spectacle

As fall creeps into the Finger Lakes, and the days shorten and the nights grow cool, the deciduous trees cast off their cloaks of green anonymity and proclaim the individuality of their species in new costumes of blazing colors. The sugar maples with their red, orange, and yellow leaves, often all on the same tree, are the most brilliant. Blending in with yellow are the poplars, beeches, and sycamores. The hickories add splashes of gold and the oaks russet. The compound leaves of the ash turn a deep purple. Often the earliest and brightest splashes of scarlet are on woodbine, also called Virginia creeper, a vine that climbs to the very tops of dead trees. Poison ivy climbs trees as well and has beautiful apricot-colored leaves, to be admired only from a distance.

Nature started this fall tapestry far back in summer. Most people are surprised when they learn that the brilliant colors of autumn leaves were in them all along but hidden by green chlorophyll, the chemical compound used by plants to change sunlight, carbon dioxide, and water into simple sugars which trees needs to grow. This requires other pigments to take over. Water-soluble, anthocyanin reveals itself in red and purple when an excess of rain washes the chemical to the leaf surface, changing the color.

Yellow is the leaf's basic color from the beginning. When the chlorophyll fades, the yellow pigments, xanthophyll and carotenoid are revealed. Tannins are also present and give russet leaves their color. Yellow and russet are colors little affected by rain.

Autumn in the Finger Lakes is always spectacular. It is most vibrant if there is but moderate rainfall, cool nights, and bright and sunny days. Sunlight is very important to the production of leaf sugars that make the scarlet anthocyanin.

Surprisingly, even a maple tree can be eccentric, refusing to turn red no matter how much sun it gets. As a rule, however, only a dark fall produces generally muted colors.

While deciduous trees are shedding their leaves, there is one conifer that grows around the Finger Lakes that is also changing color. The larch tree's needles turn yellow and drop, leaving a lacy silhouette of fine branches dotted with small cones.

Though an individual leaf may remain on the tree but a few days after its color peaks, the full spectacle usually lasts for several weeks, most years the showiest during the first two weeks in October.

Heavy rain, wind, a hard freeze or an early snowfall can quickly strip the colorful leaves from the trees.

You can preserve the vivid-colored leaves of autumn and use them in centerpieces or to decorate wreaths. Choose small branches with perfect leaves that have turned color. Pound the ends with a hammer to crush. Set the leafy branches upright in a container in a solution of one part glycerin to two parts hot water. Let sit for one to three weeks. When the leaves have darkened in color but are still soft and pliable, remove the branches from the solution and dry with paper towels.

Bogs

In Sherlock Holmes tales, bogs or moors were sinister places of great malevolence. Long ago in Finland, people believed that if they followed the flickers of burning peat gases (will-o'-the-wisp) through a bog they would be led to a pot of gold.

I don't know anyone personally who has seen will-o'-the-wisp (fox fire) around the Finger Lakes. However, zoology Professor L.A. Hausman of Cornell University recorded observing it at a distance of about fifteen feet while traveling over a road through a boggy woodland near Cayutaville.

Most of the bogs in the Finger Lakes area are small, formed by glacial damming of valleys. Their creation was a slow process that took hundreds or thousands of years as the stagnant ponds became filled-in with peat to form bogs.

They are not found along the lakeshores, the topography is not adapted to bog formation.

In Tompkins County there are bogs near Freeville, Mclean, and Malloryville. Much larger is Zurich Bog in Wayne County. One of the most interesting bogs in Central New York State is located at Junius, about six miles north of Waterloo.

There is a low diversity of plants in the harsh, uniform environment of a bog. However, several mosses and sedges grow nowhere else, along with many species of orchids. To compensate for the nutrient-poor environment some bog plants, among them sundews, pitcher plants, and bladderworts, devour insects.

Before modern wound treatments, peat moss from bogs was used to pack wounds. It made an ideal surgical dressing; large quantities of it were used during World War I.

Bogs are often described as "spongy" or "quaking." Anyone who has been in a bog knows they are unstable. You can think you are on solid ground only to find yourself sinking quickly when you take the next step. You may have difficulty freeing yourself. Perhaps your first thought is "quicksand!" And you may be right.

True quicksand is a mass of smooth, fine, round-edged particles of sand so separated by constantly moving water that the sand will not support any weight. It is usually found in hollows at the mouths of large rivers or along flat stretches of streams or beaches where pools of water become partly filled with sand, and where a layer of stiff clay beneath prevents drainage. Some areas in a bog sometimes act like true quicksand.

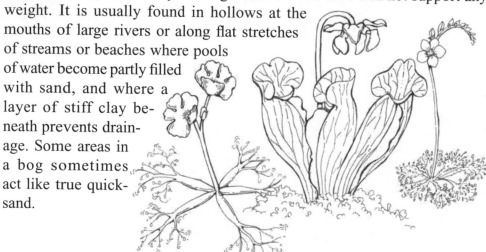

Fiction and folklore aside, if you find yourself sinking, don't panic, but remain motionless. Usually you will stop sinking when the sand reaches almost to your armpits. Then, with slow swimming motions, holding your feet still, try to ease your body into a horizontal position. You should be able to roll to firm ground. If you have a companion with you, have that person poke a branch or pole into the quicksand to break the vacuum that is sucking you down.

To get the most out of a bog experience, it is best to go with a group of naturalists with an experienced leader. It's also good from a safety stand-point. Besides the quicksand factor, you can easily get lost in a bog. There are a number or nature centers around the Finger Lakes, which can put you in touch with the appropriate people.

The Primitive Opossum

'Possums, as they are commonly called, are fairly new to the Finger Lakes area. Originally southern residents, they wandered northward, first arriving here about 1940. Gray, with white faces and large, hairless black ears (some may be white tipped), and about the size of a house cat, only with a heavier body and shorter legs, they usually live in farming areas where they find shelter beneath outbuildings or brushpiles, in old dens or in hollow logs.

'Possums are among the most primitive of animals having survived basi-cally unchanged for millions of years.

With long—nine-to-twenty-inch—rat-like tails, pointed noses, gaping mouths, large, beady eyes, and ragged teeth, opossums are not the most charismatic of animals.

They were once were hunted for their pelts. Like some other animals, they have two coats of fur, a soft inner one and an outer one that is long and coarse.

141

It's not unusual to see a 'possum with almost no tail and with its thin ears partly gone due to them having been frozen off.

Don't be surprised if you see one of these animals in a tree. With its prehensile tail and long, clawed toes, they are good climbers. They will creep out on the branches of cherry and mulberry trees to get at the fruit.

You often see 'possums in the road at night for they are primarily nocturnal. Their diet consists mainly of fruits, eggs, nuts, small rodents, vegetable matter, insects, and carrion. Occasionally one raids a farmer's henhouse.

Solitary except during the actual mating, encounters between 'possums usually result in hisses, growling, screeching, and even bitter fighting.

'Possums have one to two litters a year. After but a thirteen day gestation period, the female gives birth to up to fourteen young, each weighing about one-fifteenth of an ounce, about the size of a honeybee. The entire litter would fit into a teaspoon. Reaching the mother's pouch, a journey of three inches, with its life sustaining nipples is no easy task for the babies. They literally have to swim through her fur. Only about half of them make it.

At ten weeks the babies are about the size of mice. Their eyes are open, and they leave the fur-lined pouch for short excursions. Until they are old enough to fend for themselves — about fourteen weeks —they ride on the mother's back. She is a patient carrier though it must be difficult to climb with so heavy a load. During this period, the young return to their mother's pouch to rest and sleep.

'Possums are prey for foxes, coyotes, hawks, and owls, and many are killed on highways. They are also susceptible to parasitic disease. "Playing 'possum" is a saying based on animal behavior. When threatened, an opossum feigns death by going limp, closing its eyes and drawing its lips back in a very realistic death grin. The act saves it from predators, which only attack live prey.

If you catch an oppossum by surprise, it takes a belligerent stance, hissing, mouth agape displaying fifty fearsomely sharp teeth. Because it is nocturnal, confrontations with humans are rare.

Biologists consider opossums "slow-witted" not only because of their primitive behavior, but because their brains are small and simple in structure in comparison with other animals of approximate size. A cat, for instance, has a brain five times as large.

Opossums are the only marsupial, pouched animal in North America.

Aurora Borealis (Northern Lights)

Sometime when you are outside at night, away from bright lights, you may see the Aurora Borealis, or Northern Lights. On average, in the Finger Lakes area, there is a display about twenty times a year.

The Aurora takes many forms and colors. In our area it is usually white with a greenish tinge, occasionally with a yellowish or reddish cast. Nearer the poles the colors are much more brilliant.

Around the Finger Lakes it can appear as a ghostly moving glow, or it can fill the northern sky with brilliance. The lights may resemble searchlight beams, or flashes of distant lightning. Often they dim, then brighten.

Ever capricious, the lights can take on a corona form whereby rays seem to meet overhead in a star-like shape. Or they may look like draperies, vertical rays which rise from curving bands, and sway like heavy curtains moved by the breeze. They also may be flashes of brilliance which constantly ripple upward like tongues of flame. Occasionally they arch, like a rainbow.

Though a night spectacle, the Aurora Borealis originates in the sun, specifically with sunspots. Sunspots are a sort of boiling out or release of energy from within the sun. They may last for only a few days or for two months or more. They increase in number, then diminish through a regular cycle, which runs about twenty-one and one-fifth years.

Every sunspot spews out a vast stream of electrified particles, mainly fast-moving electrons with a few slow-moving protons. These cause atoms of the thin upper atmosphere to glow. This is the aurora. The earth's magnetic field deflects most of the particles into areas around the geomagnetic poles where the auroras are most frequent and most brilliant.

Though it can occur at any time during the year, in the Finger Lakes, the Aurora is most common in spring and fall when the earth is most nearly in line with zones of the sun where sunspots are large and frequent. Many sunspots make for many brilliant auroras.

Fossils

Since June 27, 1989, when Governor Cuomo signed the law, New York State has had an official state fossil, the eurypterid, chosen because it is unique to New York State's sedimentary rocks. The eurypterid is exceedingly rare worldwide, and is found in only five other states in the U.S. They were formed some 260 to 600 million or years ago in a sea about eight times larger than New York State. They are locally abundant in Bertie Dolostone (limestone with a high magnesium content) found in Wayne, Ontario, Seneca, and Cayuga counties in the Finger Lakes region.

The largest arthropod known, the eurypterid had a scorpion-like exoskeleton with a broad head, large compound eyes, twelve movable body segments, and a stinger-like tail. It was related to the present horseshoe crab, and more distantly to scorpions and spiders.

Other fossils, clams, corals, snails, crinoids, trilobites, and brachiopods are common in the shale that lines the gorges of the Finger Lakes. One of the best places to find these ancient relics is in a hillside of loose shale on the left side of the Portland Point Road on the east side of Cayuga Lake.

Scuba divers can see a 400-million-year-old garden of fossilized "horn coral," as eurypterid is sometimes known, near the south shore of Skaneateles Lake. Shaped like a goat's horn, the coral dates from the Devonian period when New York State was a sea bed.

Because materials in the mortar came from fossil-rich local quarries, you can even see fossils in the walls of some buildings in the City of Ithaca, particularly in the First Baptist Church, the old Home Dairy, and the Tompkins County Trust Company.

Grapes

From late August throughout October, it is harvest time in the Finger Lakes. Winery workers are busy picking, sorting, and pressing over forty varieties of grapes that will become the next bottle of wine on your table.

While wild grapes have always grown in the Finger Lakes, the native Catawba, Concord, and Isabella grapes were not suitable for making fine wine. The European vinifera grapes were not hardy enough to survive the harsh winters of New York State's Finger Lakes region. Dr. Konstantin Frank, a Ukranian immigrant and specialist in grape growing, joined forces with Charles Fournier of the Great Western Vineyards. Dr. Frank grafted the vinifera with a hardier, disease resistant rootstock that would survive cold winters and viola, the wine industry of the Finger Lakes was off and running!

The grape varieties grown today include Viniferas such as Chardonnay, Pinot Gris, Merlot, and Pinot Noir; French-American Hybrids such as Seyval Blanc and Cayuga White, Baco Noir and Marechal Foch and Labruscas (Native American) such as Catawba, Niagara and Concords and Steuben.

Many of the wineries, there are over seventy, have tours, tastings, gift shops, restaurants. A few even have overnight accommodations.

145

NOVEMBER

November is usually the grayest month of the year around the Finger Lakes. Frequently, the first significant snowfall of the year occurs in November. But there is still color if you look for it. The bare branches of the witch hazel burst forth with yellow blossoms. Winterberry have shed their leaves to reveal masses of orange-red berries, and underfoot are the tiny, bright, red-crested lichen, also called British Soldiers. In the woods and hedgerows the wild male turkeys are gobbling.

Handy Witch Hazel

Witch hazel is a compact native shrub or small tree from five-to-fifteen-feet tall, and grows freely in woods, thickets, and hedgerows throughout the Finger Lakes Region.

In late fall after the deciduous trees and shrubs have lost their leaves and become dormant, the bare twigs of witch hazel burst into bloom. The flowers are bright yellow with petals that resemble small twisted straps.

With the appearance of the flowers, the hard brown capsules clustered at the leaf bases, which hold the fruit from the previous autumn's bloom, burst open, explosively shooting out shiny black seeds. Sometimes they are propelled up to twenty feet from the plant, hence it is also known as shooting hazel.

Witch hazel blooms are quite long-lasting; it's not unusual to find them encapsulated in the ice of early winter: the reason for yet another name, winterbloom.

Long before the arrival of the colonists, native Americans were using a fluid extracted from the branches of witch hazel to treat sprains and bruises, to relieve hemorrhoids and stop hemorrhages, to alleviate skin irritations, and as a mouthwash.

The native Americans passed their knowledge on to the white man, and to this day witch hazel is a common home remedy, available in any drug-store. An astringent, it is also an ingredient in many of today's after shave lotions.

Witch hazel must be harvested only during the months when it is bare of leaves. Cutting the branches doesn't kill the bush, but it does take consider-able time for it to grow back.

In addition to its value as a pharmaceutical, the branches of witch hazel are prized for use as "divining rods" by dowsers to locate underground water for drilling wells.

A hard and heavy wood, weighing about forty-three pounds per cubic foot, witch hazel is used occasionally in the manufacture of furniture, picture frames, and musical instruments. It makes especially good handles for tools and broomsticks.

One wonders how the plant got its name. Was it because it was used by "water witchers" (dowsers)? Because witches ride on broomsticks? Or was it because British colonists mistook it for the witch-elm of their native land.

The Lichen

Nobody knows for sure how long lichens have been on earth, but they are believed to be older than the redwoods. Through the ages they have gone through few revolutionary changes. They can exist where there is no plant cover, growing slowly, making their own food using small amounts of water and carbon dioxide from the air and inorganic salts from rocks.

Several lichens are common around the Finger Lakes, but they are tiny and easily overlooked. Red-crested lichen, also called British Soldiers, one of the smallest, is the most colorful. It grows mostly on decomposing wood. Though only about one-half inch tall, the tiny clusters of bright red fruiting tops are quite spectacular.

Reindeer lichen is one you'll easily recognize. It is light gray and many-branched, like reindeer antlers.

If you pick reindeer lichen when it is dry and brittle, and put it into water, it quickly expands into a quite pretty sponge-like plant.

Another aptly named lichen, the goblet-shaped, is pale gray-green. It grows to about one-half inch tall.

Slightly taller and, again aptly named, is the pagoda lichen. It is similar in color to the goblet and has several small inverted cups up its stem.

Good places to look for lichens are along trails on public lands and on rocks in the old stone quarries around the Finger Lakes.

The Deer — White-tailed

There are a lot of white-tailed deer throughout the entire Finger Lakes Region. They are the largest animals you will see in the wild in our area. A full-grown buck can weigh between 100 and 250 pounds.

During the winter deer yard together near a food supply, often in woods bordering a cornfield or vineyard where there are ample gleanings. They also feed on winter wheat, clover, alfalfa, bark, and twigs.

There is a negative side to our large deer population. They are a serious road hazard because they have no fear of automobiles. Deer-car accidents are frequent, particularly at night.

During winters when snowfall is heavy and other food is not available, deer nibble the twigs and buds of trees. Some years the damage is severe, especially to fruit trees.

In early summer the bucks start to grow antlers. They are covered with brown velvet, which will cover and protect them until fall when the horns harden. As rutting season approaches, the velvet loosens and becomes tattered. Walking through the woods in late October you sometimes see shreds of it on saplings where a buck has scraped it off. If the bark is worn off you know he has been honing his antlers in preparation for the inevitable battles during the rut.

Bucks shed their antlers when there is a significant drop in their testosterone levels, usually soon after the rutting season. The next season's antlers may have more or fewer "points." A buck's antler points increase yearly until they are about six years old when they begin to decrease slowly over the rest of his years.

It is extremely rare to find a set of shed antlers as they are quickly consumed by rodents, beetles, and other creatures of the forest.

Seneca White Deer

Traveling either NYS Route 96 between Ovid and Geneva, or NYS 414 between Ovid and Waterloo, especially just before dusk, you could very likely see one of the most exotic animals in the entire Finger Lakes Region: the Seneca White Deer. Not a true albino because of their brown eyes, but a color variant of the native white-tailed deer, these unique animals are found almost exclusively within the boundaries of the former United States Seneca Army Depot, an ammunition storage area constructed in 1941 at the beginning of World War II.

Situated in a rural area, the Depot's eleven thousand acres were once home to a variety of wildlife. The eight-foot high security fence that completely surrounded the facility trapped inside the creatures unable to climb or fly out, and kept those on the outside from getting in.

During the first ten years little inbreeding occurred among the deer. Then in 1951, a pure white buck was spotted on the Depot grounds. Each succeeding spring yielded more fawns. By the time the first white deer was found dead of natural causes in 1956, the white deer population was well-established.

More than 2,000 brown and white deer lived within the confines of the Depot by 1956. In an effort to keep the herd population under control, the New York State Conservation Department instituted live trapping. Their efforts proved ineffective at slowing the birth rate of new fawns.

A study of the white deer was eventually initiated by the Conservation Department. Using tranquilizer guns to pacify the animals, they fitted each deer with identity collars. Forty-six of the animals received them and were studied for five years.

Eventually, a hunting program was implemented. Wildlife biologists took tissue, blood, and urine samples from animals harvested during the hunt. The research indicated that the bucks were the principal carriers of the white gene. When white bucks mated with brown does, over ninety-four percent of the resulting fawns were white. When brown bucks mated with white does, the percentage was almost exactly reversed. It was also noted that when a brown doe had twins, one could be white, while the other could be brown.

The Seneca White Deer are unique. It is estimated that over two hundred of them roam the Depot. Recently the army closed the base, recommending that 8,300 acres be turned into a "large conservation area to protect this wildlife."

A Brilliant Splash of Color

Inevitably as the brilliant colors of October fade, the gray of November creeps over the Finger Lakes. However, nature treats us to one more brilliant splash of color before winter settles in. In swales and along the margins of damp woods, you can see dense patches of scarlet as the dark green leaves of winterberry shrubs wither and fall, revealing the dark, twisted branches with their clusters of bright red berries. Actually, the berries start to ripen in August and are crimson by October, but are obscured by the shrub's own persistent leaves, and overshadowed by other blazing fall colors.

Winterberry is a holly, native to our area, but unlike its southern relatives it does not have prickly evergreen leaves. The flowers are small, greenish-white and unprepossessing. A winterberry plant is either male or female, and only the female has berries. It blooms in June.

In early winter mice scamper up the branches, take berries back to their burrows where they remove the small seeds and eat them. The fruit is classified as a food for all wildlife, but apparently it doesn't rate high on the wildlings' menus because the berries remain on the branches through the first snows of winter.

Winterberry is not meant to be picked and used for decoration as the berries will shrivel and fall from the branches almost immediately. It is a protected species, you can be arrested and fined if you are caught picking it.

The Wild Turkey

The reintroduction of the wild turkeys in the Finger Lakes Region is a real conservation success story. For many decades not one could be found anywhere in the area. Then, in the mid-1960s, the New York State Department of Conservation brought trapped turkeys from other areas where they were abundant and reestablished them here. Now you can often see flocks of them wandering beside roads, scampering through the woods, and feeding in fields. They eat insects, seeds, berries, and tender plants. Even if you don't see them, you can often hear a loud gobble, gobble, and can be sure there are male turkeys nearby. They aren't called gobblers without a reason.

The largest game bird around the Finger Lakes, a big tom turkey is a handsome, stately fellow weighing up to thirty-five pounds and about four feet tall. His plumage is greenish bronze with a gold and coppery reflection and black-tipped feathers. A long bristly "beard" dangles from the center of his chest. There are spurs on his feet. The head and neck are bare, wrinkled, and reddish mottled with blue.

152

Female turkeys are smaller and their plumage duller than the males.

Turkeys are capable of an almost vertical take-off, and biologists have clocked their flight speed at thirty-eight to forty-five miles per hour for short distances. However, a turkey prefers walking or running to flying. On the ground it can sprint faster than all but the best human runners, but even on land its endurance is poor.

Soon after the Revolutionary War, our forefathers were looking for a bird for our national emblem. The wild turkey was very much in contention, but it lost out to the bald eagle.

In the early twentieth century there was a popular dance to ragtime music called the "Turkey Trot." It was supposed to be an imitation of the jakes (male turkeys) strutting to attract the females. How realistic it was is subject to question. Turkeys do strut. However, it seems to be the spreading of their magnificent fan tail feathers along with the strut that impresses the hens.

Ten-month-old hens nest along with their older sisters. Though some juvenile males breed, most of the hens are bred by older, bearded toms. Unlike many other birds, wild turkeys do not live as pairs; the males have flocks of females.

The hen lays a clutch of twelve or so off-white eggs in a shallow nest concealed under brush; often at the base of a tree. Sometimes the eggs are found and devoured by foxes, skunks, or raccoons. Many of the young poults fall victim to these predators too, as well as to hawks and owls.

In the evening, turkeys fly to a favorite roosting place to spend the night. They prefer trees overhanging water where they are safe from foxes, coyotes, and other enemies.

Wild turkeys are native only to North and Central America.

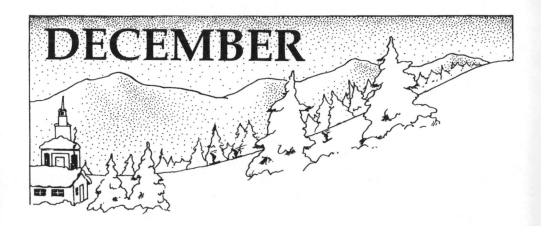

DECEMBER

Around the Finger Lakes, December usually brings cold and snowy weather. At the time of the winter solstice, about the twentieth, the average high temperature is thirty-three degrees Fahrenheit; the average low nineteen.

While many of the wild creatures have migrated to warmer climates or gone to sleep, many small mammals are busily tunneling under the snow, gnawing the roots and bark of bushes, plants, and trees. The presence of some of the larger animals such as the fox is evident by the footprints they leave in the snow, often alongside those of a hapless cottontail.

Trees are still a dominant part of the Finger Lakes' landscape, especially the evergreens. To many folks, any evergreen tree is a "pine." Some go so far as to name their businesses "Three Pines," "Twin Pines," or "Lone Pine" when the "pines" growing on the property actually may be spruce, cedar, fir, or juniper.

The most important evergreen around the Finger Lakes in December is, of course, the "Christmas" tree, chosen in early times because people looked upon the green tree as a symbol that nature did not die under the ice and snow. There are many native species of evergreens, especially in the ravines near the lakes and in the Finger Lakes National Forest in Schuyler County, which are decorated for the holiday season.

Larch

Though it has needles and cones like the evergreens that grow around the Finger Lakes, the larch is a deciduous tree. In the Fall its needles turn golden and fall from the branches. Most of our larch trees did not originate in the area; they were planted.

Larch are uniform in growth and symmetrical, their branches delicate; the wood hard and durable. In ancient times it often was used for coffins. A single tree was hollowed out to hold the body. Recently, archeologists working a dig in southern Siberia discovered two 2,400-year-old burial chambers. One 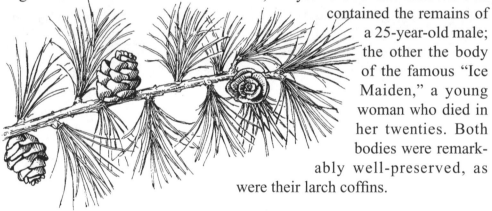 contained the remains of a 25-year-old male; the other the body of the famous "Ice Maiden," a young woman who died in her twenties. Both bodies were remarkably well-preserved, as were their larch coffins.

The Enduring Cougar

What would your reaction be if someone told you he, or she, had just seen a cougar somewhere around the Finger Lakes? Shock? Disbelief? Would you be tempted to ask, "What had you been drinking?" Well, you might want to rethink your response. Farmers, teachers, a nurse, hunters, joggers, golfers,

155

and others have said they have seen cougars, also called panthers, pumas, mountain lions, catamounts, and painters in our area

It would seem that it would be hard to mistake a cougar for any other animal. Just its size should be a clue. Next to the jaguar of South America, the cougar is the largest of all American cats. A mature male, with a body measuring from four-to-five-and-one-half-feet, plus a tail two-to-three-feet long, weighs about 150 pounds. The female is somewhat smaller. The animal's tail is distinctive too, not bushy like that of a fox; more slender and curling at the bottom. A cougar can be tawny or black. At least three of the people who told me they've seen one of these cats have said they were black. In fact, they called them black panthers.

A cougar matures in two to three years. After a gestation period of three months, the female gives birth to three (usually) kittens. Their life expectancy is about eight years. The kits are covered with spots and stripes, which soon give way to their tawny coats. Strictly carnivores, at four months the babies are weaned to meat. If given the chance, male cougars often kill the young.

In early times, cougars ranged from ocean to ocean and from Canada south to Patagonia. Fearful pioneers saw them as fierce, treacherous beasts; bloodthirsty killers of small domestic animals. So the government jumped in, offering bounties on them, and soon cougars disappeared from all but the wildest portions of the West.

A few decades ago, however, substantial numbers of the cats were back in Grand Canyon National Park and in Kaibab National Park where hunting cougars was prohibited. When experts wildlife realized the cougars were decimating the deer population, they again opened up the parks to the hunting of cougars. The result was an explosion of the deer population, the deer consuming more forage than the park could produce. Hunting of deer was instituted and that of cougars again forbidden. The big cats resumed their ancient function of keeping the deer herd under control.

I called the Department of Environmental Conservation in Cortland to see if they knew of any recent cougar sightings in our area. The man with whom I spoke said he knew of no confirmed sightings, but he thinks it likely there are some around. He gives credence to one report of a sighting December 18, 2001, in the Binghamton area. He is puzzled, though, by the fact there have been no reports of domestic animal kills, especially sheep. Is it possible that wild prey is so available that a cougar doesn't have to come near human habitation? Also, a single cougar has a range of up to sixty square miles — not exactly a dense population, they feed mostly early in the morning and at dusk, sleeping during the day.

According to the Seneca Sheriffs Department, more people seem to have heard cougars than to have seen them. Over the past twenty years or so, police agencies have received calls from frightened lake residents along the west shore of Cayuga Lake who heard what they thought was a panther traveling from north to south through the ravine-furrowed woods behind their cottages. They described its cry as a blood-curdling scream like that of a woman in mortal terror. Whether it was a cougar or not remains a mystery.

If you think you have seen a cougar, the people at the DEC want to hear from you. They won't laugh at you, but they will come and look for things like paw prints, tufts of fur and scratches in the bark of a tree where the animal may have exercised its claws.

Fox

Fox are burrowing animals and live in underground dens. Usually they hide by day and hunt by night. Birds and small animals make up their main diet. Occasionally they also eat frogs, fish, insects, and berries. In earlier times they were a nuisance, often raiding farmers' henhouses.

There are two kinds of fox in the Finger Lakes area: the red and the gray. The red far outnumbers the gray. The red fox has a sleek, burnished gold coat of fur long-prized in the fur trade. The red fox's beauty has been its undoing. It used to be shot, trapped, even poisoned for its pelt.

The male red fox grows to a length of forty-one inches including its sixteen-inch bushy tail. The upper part of its body is reddish yellow, the underparts and the tip of its tail white. The feet and forelegs are black.

Folktales—and there are many—credits the fox's survival to its stealth and guile.

With legs slightly longer than those of the red, the gray fox ranges from the Atlantic to the Pacific and South to Texas. It is of low rank in the fur trade.

The young are born in the spring in litters of from three to nine. Foxes are active all year.

The Shrews

There are about seven species of shrews living in the Finger Lakes Region. Mouse-sized with tiny bead-like eyes, ears concealed or nearly so, it is often difficult to distinguish between the species; our glimpses of them are usually brief. All are scrappy little bundles of energy, mostly insect-eaters, which do no harm to man.

Least Shrew

The least shrew is identified by its cinnamon color. It is about two and one-half inches in length with a short (about one-half inch) tail. It produces one litter a year.

Short-tail Shrew

The short-tail shrew is larger, three to four inches, and lead-colored. It's diet consists mostly of insects and moles. It can eat its own weight in insects, worms, snails, and other small animals each day. The eyes are so small they are barely visible and its tail is short like the least shrew's. Short-tail shrew saliva is poisonous to its prey. An indication of the animal's presence is a tunnel under the surface of the soil or in the snow. Two to three litters of from five to eight a year are usual.

Masked Shrew

The masked shrew is grayish brown and tiny, about two inches, with a bicolored tail almost as long. It is hard to tell it from the pygmy shrew, which weighs about the same as a dime and is the smallest living mammal.

Smoky Shrew

The smoky shrew is a bit larger than the masked, dull brown with a bicolored tail and pale feet. It prefers to live in birch and hemlock forests with a deep layer of leaf mold on the ground.

Long-tailed Shrew

The long-tailed shrew is about two and three quarters of an inch long, lighter underparts and a two-and-one-half-inch long tail. It is believed to have but one litter a year.

Northern Water Shrew

The northern water shrew is a large shrew, about three and one-half inches, blackish gray with a three-inch tail. It is found along cold small streams with cover on the banks and in bogs. It is a good swimmer and feeds on aquatic organisms. Little is known about its breeding habits.

The Mice
The Deer Mouse and the White-footed Mouse

The deer mouse and the white-footed mouse are hard to distinguish from each other, their differences are so slight. Their upperparts are rusty brown and their bellies and feet white. They are about the size of a house mouse, but their tails are longer and their ears bigger. The deer mouse's tail is always bicolored.

These are cute little creatures that eat seeds, nuts, and insects, and store seeds and nuts. You never know where one will pop up. They nest any place that affords shelter: in logs, stumps, underground, or in abandoned squirrel nests. It is believed these animals live two to three years in the wild and have two to four litters a year.

deer
mouse

meadow jumping mouse

Meadow Jumping Mouse

The meadow jumping mouse is one of the three true hibernators around the Finger Lakes, the other two being the woodchuck and the bat. These animals do not eat, urinate or defecate during their entire period of hibernation. The other deep sleepers rouse periodically.

The meadow jumping mouse is olive colored with a dark olive back and white belly. It is easily recognized by its long hindlegs, large hindfeet, and extremely long tail. Because it is primarily nocturnal it is not often seen.

From October or November to April or May it sleeps in a nest two to three feet beneath the surface of the ground in a well-drained location. The female gives birth to four to five babies two to three times a year.

The woodland jumping mouse is distinguished from the meadow by a white tip on its tail. It is not common in the Finger Lakes area.

The Voles

A vole is in the same family as the common house mouse. Like mice, they are rapid multipliers with voracious appetites. They are cyclical, sometimes appearing in huge enough numbers to do serious damage to trees and grain crops. Then, unaccountably, they all but disappear. You see few of them after heavy rains.

When their population becomes great enough to threaten trees and grain, agriculturists often fumigate to get rid of them. Organic farmers sometimes turn swine into an area to root up their nests and burrows. Most years they are kept under control by natural predators: foxes, raccoons, skunks, opossums, coyotes, weasels, owls, crows, herons, gulls, hawks, and snakes.

Meadow Voles

Meadow voles are small rodents weighing up to two and one-half ounces, brownish or grayish with light tan colored undersides. Their short ears are concealed by fur. They are a bit larger than the other two species of voles common around the Finger Lakes; up to five inches in length with a tail from one and one-half inches to two and one-half inches long. They have small beady eyes.

Meadow voles inhabit low moist areas and orchards with grass undergrowth where they eat seeds, grain, grasses, clover, and roots. Sometimes they girdle the trees. They are territorial and prolific.

Red-backed Voles

Red-backed voles are forest rodents. They average about four and one-half inches in length with a tail one and one-quarter to two inches long. Weighing around an ounce they usually have reddish backs and gray sides. Their two-inch-long tails are grey and tan in color.

Pine Voles

Pine voles are rather handsome little critters rarely found around the Finger Lakes in stands of pines as the name suggests. Here they live mostly in deciduous forests and in orchards. In the south, however, they do live in pine forests. Pine voles are small, usually about three and one-half inches, auburn colored with small ears. You can tell them from the red-backed and meadow voles by their short tails, which are not over an inch long.

In orchards pine voles may burrow around trees and eat the bark from roots. They also feed on bulbs, tubers, and seeds. They produce three to four litters of three to four young (usually) a year.

Beneath the Surface — The Moles

Moles live most of their lives beneath the surface of the ground. Their presence is usually apparent in low ridges of soil they push up with their pig-like snouts in yards, gardens, golf courses, and meadows. Their spade-like feet are also used in burrowing. They damage lawns and golf courses but they also eat many insects and aerate the soil. Besides insects, moles eat worms and some vegetable matter.

Moles are not prolific breeders usually having only one litter a year of between three to seven young. Naked at birth, the babies are independent at about one month but do not breed until they are one year old.

Eastern Moles

Eastern moles are larger than shrews and voles, measuring from four-and-one-half-to-six-and-one-half-inches. Their tails are comparatively short, one to one-and-one-half-inches long. They have no external ears, and their tiny eyes are covered with a thin layer of skin leading some people to believe, incorrectly, that all moles are blind.

The Finger Lakes eastern mole is slate colored, with a naked tail and front feet broader than they are long. It has a naked, pointed snout. It prefers moist, sandy loam, shunning soil that is extremely dry.

Star-nosed Moles

Star-nosed moles are somewhat smaller than the Eastern; four to five inches in length, but with a longer tail (three to three and one-half inches). Its distinguishing feature is its nose, which is surrounded by twenty-two finger-like, flesh-colored projections giving it the appearance of a star. Its eyes are very small but apparent. Like the Eastern, the star-nosed has front feet as broad as they are long.

This mole likes low, wet ground near water for its home. It is a good swimmer, often seen in water or wandering around aboveground. It feeds on worms and insects, particularly aquatic ones. With poor eyesight and sense of smell, it finds food with the sensitive tentacles on its snout.

Star-nosed moles are often gregarious so where you see one there are probably more. Like the meadow vole, star-nosed have one litter a year, sometimes a second in late summer.

Almanac Index

THE AUTHOR

Margaret Miller was born in Canandaigua, New York, and has lived all her life in the Finger Lakes area, most recently between Seneca and Cayuga Lakes where she has worked as a licensed New York State real estate broker.

From her mother, a self-taught naturalist, she inherited a keen interest in and appreciation for the beautiful and intriguing things she saw all around her. This love of nature encouraged Margaret to write this book.

For two years Margaret's column, *Nature Notes*, appeared weekly in the Trumansburg Free Press, the Interlaken Review, and the Ovid Gazette.

THE ILLUSTRATOR

Sheri Amsel has written and illustrated more than 25 books exploring nature and science topics. With degrees in botany, zoology, anatomy, and biomedical illustration, Sheri has gone on to work on writing and illustrating children's and adult's nature books, school and library workshops, outdoor education, nature trail development, and teaching college science.

Sheri works out of her home studio in the Adirondack Mountains. www.adirondackillustrator.com.